WHITENESS

W H I T E N E S S

ROOM 5 NUMBER 01

Editor: John Tercier

Production: Christopher Hight
Lorens Holm
Mark Morris

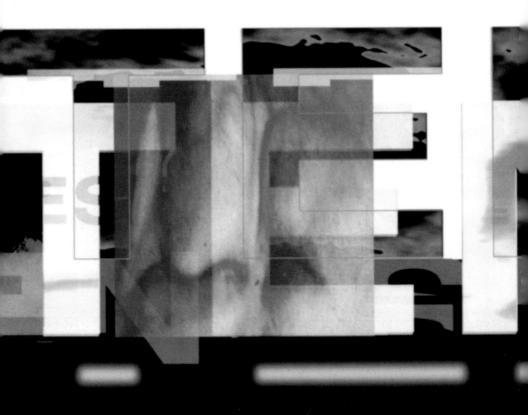

Editorial Office and Subscription Information:
The London Consortium
Institute of Contemporary Arts
12 Carlton House Terrace
London SW1Y 5AH

First published in the United Kingdom in 2000 by
Lawrence & Wishart.
144a Old South Lambeth Road
London SW8 1XX

ISSN: 1472-1066

Printed in Great Britain by Cambridge University
Press, Cambridge

ROOM 5

THE LONDON CONSORTIUM

Room 5 is the journal of the London Consortium. It documents the research activities of the Consortium and provides a forum for new work.

The London Consortium is an innovative, multi-disciplinary, postgraduate research programme associated with Birkbeck College — University of London, the Architectural Association School of Architecture, the Institute for Contemporary Arts and the Tate Gallery. It awards Masters and Doctorate degrees in Cultural Studies and Humanities.

Architectural
Association

the london

TATE

No other Masters or PhD programme in the world offers to its students the resources of a major international art gallery and museum, one of the world's most famous arts centres, a renowned university, and the cutting-edge Architectural Association.

These resources are matched by the intellectual ambitions of the London Consortium, which provides a rigorous, challenging and exhilarating programme of study leading to either a Masters or PhD degree in the Humanities and Cultural Studies. The Master of Research degree entails coursework and a dissertation, the PhD degree coursework and a thesis. Both programmes lead to a degree of the University of London.

As befits the four participating institutions, the courses provide a mixture of the most rigorous academic argument with the opportunity to test those studies against the work of institutions that make cultural policy decisions on a daily basis.

The Consortium has an internationally distinguished regular and visiting faculty. Students will be taught by an extraordinary range of leading scholars and practitioners, ranging from architectural theorists and designers through specialists in art history and curatorial work, to cinema critics and filmmakers and historians, literary scholars, artists, political theorists and philosophers.

All students will automatically have privileged access to the event programmes and resources of the four participating institutions, including Tate Gallery exhibitions; ICA cinema screenings, Talks, Exhibitions, Live Arts and New Media Programme; Architectural Association exhibitions.

For more information, please contact:
London Consortium Administrator
ICA
12 Carlton House Terrace
London SW1Y 5AH
United Kingdom

telephone: +44 020 7839 8669
fax: +44 020 7930 9896
email: loncon@ica.org.uk
http: www.bbk.ac.uk/consortium

ICA
SUPPORTED BY
Sun microsystems
Institute of Contemporary Arts

CONTENTS

If Hegel was right and the owl of history flies only at dusk, then it seems only appropriate that in the nineties 'whiteness' began to be the subject of sustained intellectual and academic interrogation rather than, as was too often the case, the unexamined framework of enquiry. Perhaps it could not be otherwise, given the rise of race and gender studies within the academy, themselves a complex cause and effect of larger shifts within western societies, which made whiteness as the unexamined norm much less sustainable. A novel such as Hanif Kureishi's The Black Album, precipitated by the aftermath of Rushdie's The Satanic Verses, and referencing Prince's Black Album, set up a dialogue with both The Beatles White Album (designed by the English artist Richard Hamilton) and with Joan Didion's 1968 collection White Album, and made visible the possible 'race' implications of earlier 'white' work.

But if the 'visibility of whiteness' in nineties work led to a reinterrogation of the past – a variation on Eliot's dictum that every new work changes our perception of what precedes it – it also called into question the adequacy of finding the politics of race inscribed in every example of whiteness, at all times and all places. Could such a reading be sustained in the face of Robert Ryman's 'white' painting, as it could with D.W. Griffiths' The Birth of a Nation? Or in the face of Satie's 'white music'. The more the centrality of whiteness across a range of practices became clear, the clearer became the difficulty of offering one interpretative paradigm for all 'white works'. What other than a generalised preoccupation with whiteness bound together Mallarmé's Un Coup de Des, Le Corbusier's white buildings and Whistler's Symphony In White? Perhaps it was a question of trying to identify a historical horizon for this preoccupation – let's say the late nineteenth century and the emergence of early modernism. But clearly, this was not adequate since 'whiteness' was not limited to the twentieth century. Yet the end of the nineteenth and the beginning of the twentieth century did seem to mark an intensification of concern.

These are just a few of the ruminations that precipitated the course on Whiteness, part of the postgraduate programme of The London Consortium, a partnership between the ICA, the Architectural Association, the Tate Gallery and Birkbeck College, University of London. The Whiteness course grew initially out of conversations with Sunil Khilnani of Birkbeck College. I had been writing on national identity across a ten year period and he was preparing a major biography on Nehru – it was our common fascination with whiteness and our ignorance of how to find a language to address whiteness in all its variousness that led us to devise the course. We were joined by Gordana Korolija, an architect affiliated with the Architectural Association, as a triumvirate, who, with the students across a five year span, thought and rethought what might count as an adequate account of whiteness in the cultural practices of the twentieth century.

This collection edited by the students of the course is testimony to the variety of attempts made upon the subject – the model might be Stevens' Thirteen Ways of Looking at a Blackbird – and ought properly to be dedicated to all those who took part in the seminars and the larger enterprise. In their way these essays might help to see why sometimes we may feel the need to reformulate one of Marx' famous theses on Feurbach: it is first necessary to understand the world in order to change it.

Philip Dodd
Director
Institute of Contemporary Arts
London

INTRODUCTION

The papers in this volume explore 'Whiteness' as quality, phenomenon, symbol in film, photography, art, music, and architecture. There are areas of convergence: race, history, Modernism, hygiene, but there is also motion outwards, towards the boundaries, into dirt, notoriety, deviance, and death. Perhaps the use of white is entirely arbitrary; perhaps it only carries the meanings we inscribe upon its unmarked surface. These essays, however, make the claim that within certain bounds, and at certain levels of function, arbitrary choice ceases and whiteness itself, what it is and what it has become, inscribes on its own blank surface the reality of the ideal of the immaculately white.

Where lies the phenomenon of whiteness's perfection? Is white, white all the way through or just on the surface? Diana Yeh dissects the work of Steve McQueen in an attempt to find where whiteness might lie. She poses the question of whether the political correctness of responding to his art in purely formal terms is not merely a 'whitening' of the work on a political level. Yeh sees McQueen's film technique less as employing blackness undefined by whiteness, but, rather, as containing whiteness within itself. By doing this, she asserts that McQueen reclaims the aesthetic quality of blackness and whiteness from politics.

Charles Rice also looks below the surface in his examination of the historical relationship of black-and-white and colour photography. He questions the contemporary relationship between whiteness and photography by defining whiteness not as technique, but as an exercise in language. For him, colour articulates the underlying subject upon the photographic surface.

A surface, made empty by whiteness, is a challenge to our own shortcomings. It dares us to leave our mark. David Tang explores, in the 1948 film Scott of the Antarctic, the compulsion to inscribe, to chart and to name: to make black marks upon white surfaces. Scott's physical journey across the Antarctic snows is condensed into an inscribed line invading the blankness of his journal pages. The film uses this convention and projects it back onto the landscape, the journey, and the desire of men to inscribe meaning onto nature through an act of will. Unsullied whiteness is a danger that invites transgression.

The retribution that whiteness exacts for this violation is the theme of John Tercier's return to that same film Scott of the Antarctic. Tercier questions the Modernist assumption that the relationship of meaning to symbol is arbitrary, and, via the phenomenon of the 'whiteout', brings whiteness and death together as cause and effect.

Kathy Battista examines the scandal that surrounded the exhibition of Mary Kelly's Post-Partum Document in 1976 at the Institute of Contemporary Arts. She focuses our attention on the concept of pollution and its relation to the Modernist aesthetic. In her formulation, the white cube of the gallery is a statement of power and prestige, maintaining the purity of high culture, isolating it from contagion by popular culture. She traces the gallery's development as a 'white male space' and relates this to the ways in which feminist artists have challenged its sterile rule.

Whiteness not only challenges, it also threatens. Travis Miles examines Tony Conrad's avant-garde film of 1966, The Flicker, in which the physiological phenomenon of white and black alternation, i.e. 'flicker', is manipulated to produce patterns of visual harmonic frequency. The lack of imagery and 'blankness' of The Flicker allows a spectator response that promises freedom, but then delivers a threat.

The challenge and threat of whiteness not only invites violation and violent response, it may also perpetrate its own violence. In The Beauty of Surfaces Lorens Holm photographs gallery walls – in particular the South wall of Tate Britain. This wall was damaged by German bombs in 1940, and that damage is now listed. An expanse of limestone was ravaged by a flash of white light, and then translated by light, through the medium of photography, into a sort of beauty. This is a beauty composed of the damage done by whiteness.

Whiteness, besides being that upon which a mark is set, may also obscure the mark. It may be a mask. From high culture to pop culture, from Africa to America via Japan, Mark Morris examines the cultural complexities of Michael Jackson's face. He argues that Jackson's whiteness project, condemned as a botched, race related disfigurement, is none of those things. A combination of Romanticism's ideal of epicoene masculine beauty, the tradition of European theatrical make-up, the Noh mask of the Japanese stage, and the technical imperatives of current film technique have to produced a face that is not to be read as a betrayal of race but, rather, a face loyal to the genealogy of performance.

Ruth Adams also points towards the use of whiteness in the revelations and concealments of another twentieth century icon. The white hair and white face of Andy Warhol reflected a blankness that helped maintain his mystique. In Western culture, the fact that whiteness is the norm cloaks it with invisibility. It allows the white man to attain the Enlightenment intellectual ideal, the observing subject without properties – that is to say an object. Warhol aspired to the status of a hidden object – an invisible, because white, observer. But there is a price to be paid for this cloak of invisibility; underneath it lurks the "desolate suspicion of non-existence", the erasure of subjectivity – death.

Christopher Hight, using the film Suture, explores the invisibility that whiteness extends over race. The white light, white noise, white heat of American culture are the grid, in the interstices of which the Afro-American is made invisible. Western harmonic structures create an image of order by endowing noise with form, a racially white form. The black is coded as a proportion of whiteness, a debased version of the harmonious ideal. The replacing of the analogue model of harmony by a digital model of repetition, may disrupt the harmonic ideal, but it produces naught but white noise.

Formless noise holds no liberation or power, only a living death.

Another way of using black and white in the composition of the real is found in the work of the photographer John Hilliard. Michael Uwemedimo reveals the use of white light and darkness to construct binary oppositions that set up a system of meaning. Hilliard's images challenge the casual associations of whiteness with life and blackness with death, not to silence them, but to allow them to speak even more loudly through increasingly complex oscillations of meaning.

The purity of whiteness is generally acknowledged as a thing good and to be desired. Yet many of these papers deal, in one way or other, with a threat of violence from the immaculately white. Whiteness makes invisible, but it also increases visibility. What is it that we wish both to hide and to see, to possess and to destroy, that threatens to destroy us? The authors appear to be staring into a whiteness described by Herman Melville as the:

heartless void [that] stabs us from behind with the thought of annihilation...

John Tercier

LWH

il **WHITENESS** is

Christopher Makos
Andy Warhol, Working Out with Soho Training Center
Owner, Lidija Cengic, at the Factory, New York, 1982.
Courtesy Fahey/Klein Gallery, Los Angeles, and Govinda
Gallery, Washington, D.C., ' the artist

DRELLA PLAYS THE WHITE MAN
ANDY WARHOL AND THE CONSTRUCTION OF WHITE MASCULINITY

RUTH ADAMS

Andy Warhol was perhaps the ultimate white man. He was arguably the epitome of Western cultural representations of white masculinity – yet while he drew on such stereotypes in the construction of his unique and instantly recognisable public persona, he also expanded and subverted them in subtle and complex ways.

In contrast to perhaps his most famous subject, Marilyn Monroe, the 'whitest' woman, who was used to represent nature and life, Warhol came to signify both culture and death. Images of death were both embodied by Warhol and an important trope in his work.

Dyer reports: "It is said that when sub-Saharan Africans first saw Europeans, they took them for dead people, for living cadavers. If so, it was a deadly perception, for whites may not only embody death, they also bring it."[1] The image of the white man as both dead and bringer of death may seem a fairly reasonable response from non-white peoples who may have experienced the ravages of imperialism and colonialism, but this is an image far more entrenched in white, Western culture; perhaps as the inverse of the supposed fearsome fecundity of the black man. Horror literature and film often has this image of the white man at its centre, and this is a predominantly white genre. Dyer suggests that horror functions as a catharsis:

> Horror is licensed to deal with what terrifies us – partly by giving it free reign for the safe length of a movie, partly by being low, dismissible and often risible [...] It is a cultural space that makes bearable for whites the exploration of the association of whiteness with death.[2]

This association finds expression in the form of the vampire; the dead white man who feeds off and kills other white people. The association between Warhol and vampirism was one that was made regularly throughout his career. He made a film called *Dracula* and his Factory nickname was 'Drella'. Drella was an amalgam of Dracula and Cinderella and was, as Gerard Malanga recalled; "a homosexual campy fairy-tale thing like the Wicked Witch of the North. Andy was cast as the bad guy in the fairy tale."[3] These vampiric associations arose partly from Warhol's appearance. He was extremely pale and claimed to have been afflicted with vitiligo as a child. He emphasised his pallor with make-up, predominantly black clothing and possibly the most famous head of white hair since Monroe's. His Slavonic origins also added some piquancy to the comparison. While some of the Dracula comparisons were light-hearted, even affectionate, they were generally made by commentators hostile to Warhol, who found his persona and/or his work offensive. Warhol challenged many of the certainties of Modernism, and his very ambiguity and ambivalence provoked a sense of uneasiness, even the 'uncanny', in his critics. Judith Halberstam's description of the Vampire is a spookily accurate picture of Warhol:

> Dracula is otherness itself, a distilled version of all others produced by and within fictional texts, sexual science, and psychopathology. He is monster and man, feminine and powerful, parasitical and wealthy; he is repulsive and fascinating, he exerts the consummate gaze but is scrutinised in all things, he lives forever but can be killed. Dracula is indeed not simply a monster but a technology of monstrosity.[4]

Dyer argues that the vampire myth strikes so deep to the heart of the fear of white men that it must be attributed to non-mainstream whites, 'the other', such as Jews or homosexuals. The vampire bite is a metaphor for the sexual act, but, like homosexuality, it is non-reproductive; it can never result in life and therefore, by extension, must result in death.

Warhol, like Dracula, was often portrayed as parasitic. Many of these accusations arose from his relationships with his 'superstars', his Factory acolytes. Warhol's own marginalised position and his apparent lack of judgement, often taken as affirmation, resulted in a following of other marginalised individuals. His coterie comprised a motley crew of love-starved society debs, drug addicts, drag queens and wannabes, most with a variety of emotional problems. Warhol put this bunch of misfits on show; on film, on tape and in person, and when they almost inevitably self-destructed he simply kept on recording. He was reproached for exploiting other people's misery, encouraging them to spill their messed-up guts for the voyeuristic titillation of himself and whoever else cared to watch. Such accusations were not helped by claims (probably true) that he paid his stars little or nothing for their appearances while he was raking in big bucks. While Warhol was undoubtedly voyeuristic – he admitted as much – his work also suggests that we, the viewer, are equally guilty – we too keep on watching. He attributed his policy of non-interference to a liberal belief that people should be allowed to do what they want – regardless of whether it is 'good' for them. He once said that he would not have prevented Monroe from killing herself if that would have made her 'happy'.

The attempt on Warhol's life in 1968 further served to accentuate his horror film image; he literally came 'back from the dead'. Serious injury made him look even more cadaverous than ever. When he visited London in 1971, Geoffrey Matthews of the *Evening News* described him as looking like "a corpse which has somehow raised itself up off a cold stone slab and walked out of the mortuary."[5] Similarly, Richard Avedon's 1969 portrait of Andy's chest, criss-crossed with snaking scars and sutures, puts one in mind of another Hollywood horror icon – Frankenstein's Monster. Associations with death were attributed not only to the more obvious elements of Warhol's oeuvre, such as the *Death and Disaster* series, but also to his apparently more innocuous portraits of *living* people. Jonathan Flatley cites a reported incident when Jasper Johns, having seen Warhol's portrait of Holly Solomon said to her, "Hi Holly... how does it feel to be dead?"[6] Flatley reads Johns' comment as meaning that Solomon had 'died' to become an objet d'art or, less poetically, "an object, or more nearly a commodity, brand 'Warhol'."[7] This death through objectification is, Flatley argues, symptomatic of being famous. Being a public figure is rather like imagining oneself dead or attending one's own funeral. "You get to see yourself reified, eulogised, coherent, whole – and you get to see other people recognising you."[8] Given this, we might see the fact that Warhol started painting the *Marilyns* after her physical death as almost irrelevant; the paintings have as much to say about Monroe's condition during her life as after her death. However, Kirk Varnedoe argues that her death was crucial to another interpretation of the work. With reference to *Gold Marilyn* he says:

> Not only was Marilyn dead when he painted it, but the whole world she stood for was dead. That kind of peroxide, sex-bomb, movie glamour has more to do with the gleaming chrome on a 1957 Cadillac than it does with the [...] squared-off Lincoln Continental that Kennedy was shot in [...] in 1963.[9]

Alternatively, we might see Warhol's portraiture as not only 'bringer of death' but also extender of life. Flatley suggests that Warhol's work can be understood in terms of *prosopopoeia*, which he defines as "the fiction of a voice beyond the grave. It is the trope that ascribes face, name, or voice to the absent, inanimate or dead."[10] Holly Solomon clearly understood the dual functionality of Warhol's portraiture because her gloating retort to Johns was "Long after I'm dead, it will be hanging."[11] Likewise, by transforming newspaper photographs and reports into permanent works of art, Warhol prevents the unknown and largely anonymous victims of car crashes and food poisoning from simply becoming tomorrow's chip wrappers and endows them with a fame (albeit posthumously) that stretches far beyond 'fifteen minutes'.

Although Warhol perhaps empathised, and even sympathised with Monroe, more than anything he aspired to her iconic status, and perhaps even envied her a little. David Bourdon suggests that it was not so much her untimely death that excited Warhol sufficiently for him to start painting *Marilyns*, but the enormous amount of press coverage that it generated. Warhol realised fairly early in his career that if he wanted to be a star, it would not be enough to simply be an important painter, he would also have to be a 'face'. 'Warhol the artist' became an increasingly essential element of his oeuvre, some said his best work, encouraged by his 'superstars' and on the advice of Ivan Karp, who told him; "You know people want to see *you*. Your looks are a certain part of your fame – they feed the imagination."[12] Warhol set about creating a persona for public consumption inspired by Hollywood's example.

Like Monroe, Andy adopted white hair for maximum transformational effect. He started dying his hair blond shortly after his arrival in New York, but once his hair started to thin significantly he began wearing wigs. The early numbers were grey and fairly naturalistic, but he soon graduated to the, increasingly artificial looking, blond, white and silver versions that became his trademark. While, like Monroe, white/blond hair offered Warhol both transformational and attention grabbing qualities, he clearly couldn't and wouldn't want it to convey the same messages as Marilyn's blond halo. In his book *Big Hair*, McCracken traces a 'periodic table' of blondness from 'bombshell', through 'brassy' and 'sunny' to 'cool' and 'platinum'. While Marilyn's overt sexuality placed her firmly in the first category. Warhol might be said to have adapted the latter two. 'Cool' blondness is a paradox; while at first glance it suggests the same openness and access that bombshell blondness offers, this access is refused. This could be seen as symbolic of both Warhol's persona and his art. They appear glamourous, familiar and accessible at a surface level, but beyond that surface the way is blocked: "If you want to know about Andy Warhol, [he said], just look at the surface of my paintings and my films and there I am, there's nothing behind it."[13]

Warhol might also be compared with the cool blondes of Hitchcock's movies:

> it wasn't that he wanted them to forswear their sexuality on the screen, what he wanted was a tension between the sexual and the social. He wanted everyday life to be haunted by a sexuality that became all the more powerful for its annexation. Hitchcock began with blondness, the better to communicate a sexual presence, and then he directed the blondes to stand away from their sensuality. He sought to heighten sexuality by distancing it.[14]

Likewise, while Warhol did not actually forswear his sexuality, he certainly annexed it. He was not keen on physical contact, or unmediated intimacy of any sort, and therefore explored his sexuality at a voyeuristic distance. Because he was homosexual, his sexuality was also annexed by society. While the homosexual, like the vampire, is forced to look on from the sidelines, this very liminality makes their presence, whilst unseen, all the more potent and unnerving in the popular imagination.

If Warhol was undoubtedly subversive in his 'cool' blond phase, he abandoned such strategies when he moved into his later 'platinum' phase. McCracken describes platinum as "the colour of choice for society women in New York City."[15] During the late seventies and eighties this is precisely what Warhol appeared to become. The star-struck youth became a fully-fledged star and he swapped avant-garde practices for commissioned portraits, product endorsement, *Interview* magazine and nights out at Studio 54. He moved from the outside to the inside, to wealth and celebrity – and his hair reflected this change in status. Many critics of Warhol see this period as evidence of his 'selling out' and abandoning his principles. On the contrary, this apparent shift was entirely consistent within his commodity logic; Warhol always wanted to be a movie-star, a product, he was simply actualising his ambitions.

Like Monroe, Warhol was often taken to be 'dumb'. His blank stare, his glitzy, kitschy tabloid magazine paintings and his apparent inability to manage responses any more erudite than 'Gee' or 'Wow' all contributed to this image. It was often assumed of Warhol, as of Marilyn, that when they did exhibit flashes of incontestable brilliance it was more by accident than design. The truth was quite the reverse, Warhol's dumbness was part of his carefully crafted public persona; it was a blankness that maintained his mystique and resisted the fixing of all by the most ambiguous meanings to him.

Warhol's 'dumbness' might also be interpreted as related to his assertion that he wanted to be a machine. If Monroe was a sex object struggling to be taken seriously as a subject, then Warhol was a subject that aspired to be an object. In Dyer's schemata it is the fact that whiteness is taken to be the norm, and therefore unmarked and unspecific, an absence, that allows the white man to aspire to the highest point on the Enlightenment's intellectual ideal, the observing subject without properties – that is to say, an object. What fascinated Warhol about Monroe was that the real woman had effectively disappeared behind a screen of representation. This is what Warhol's multiple silk-screens of Monroe show and it also makes sense of Warhol's assertion that one only had to look at the surface of his paintings. Since what he was representing was only a surface to begin with, paradoxically the depth of the paintings lies in their very superficiality. The multiplicity of the images might be interpreted as the many subjectivities that journalists, biographers and fans tried to rehabilitate from Monroe's terminal object, which by their very nature, could never be more than superficial projections upon that object.

Given Warhol's interest in, and awareness of, Monroe's tragic condition in life and death, why would he regard her as aspirational? I would suggest because he realised what Marilyn perhaps did not; that objecthood could be a protective haven as well as a prison. If the properties of Warhol's portraiture were death and rebirth, Daniel Herwitz suggests that film has similar properties and that this was the root of Warhol's obsession with Hollywood:

> Warhol is fascinated with the film star because she dies on screen and is recast as present in an eternalised, 'living', re-presented, past. There she is both herself (with her own qualities) and the film's material. It is as if Warhol's fantasy is to die and become reborn as a film image whose life is replaced by glamour and the gaze of everybody.[16]

In a way, Warhol had found a way to have the fame cake and eat it too. The silver screen works both ways – projecting and protecting. Flatley suggests that Warhol's understanding of this process is made manifest by his casting of himself as 'The Shadow' in his *Myths* series, alongside other iconic figures such as Superman and Mickey Mouse. This painting "allegorizes Warhol's fantasy that [...] he could move into the public precisely as someone *hidden*."[17] The bigger his public profile became and the further removed from its source subject, the more it obscured and protected it. In this respect, Warhol faithfully followed his own advice, advice that he might have offered Monroe:

> You should always have a product that's not just 'you'. An actress should count up her plays and movies and a model should count up her photographs [...] and an artist should count up his pictures so you always know exactly what you're worth and you don't get stuck thinking your product is you and your fame, and your aura.[18]

Warhol is perhaps suggesting here that Monroe's tragedy was a result not perhaps of her objectification, but because she invested too much of her subject in her object and was therefore unable to maintain a necessary critical distance.

The construction of both Warhol and Marilyn's public personas were so complete that they took on lives of their own. Their public personas could be described as their 'doubles'. Doubles have a long history in Western culture and are generally portrayed as the uncanny, something to be feared. In the double the subject perceives both self and non-self, the familiar and the strange. Baudrillard makes a specific connection between the double and death. "A vengeful and vampiric double, an unquiet soul. the double begins to prefigure the subject's death, haunting him in the very midst of his life."[19] I have already outlined the links between a particular type of double, Warhol's portraits, and death; however, the double can also put something of a strain on the living subject. While Warhol felt that a portrait, a double, a public self should be as perfect as possible, he also knew that it was a hard act to live up to. No doubt playing heavily on his vampiric reputation, Warhol once said "I'm sure I'm going to look in the mirror and see nothing. People are always calling me a mirror and if a mirror looks into a mirror, what is there to see?"[20] Steven Shaviro suggests that this perhaps was what Warhol wanted to happen, if his reflection would disappear, if he could become simply an image, it would cease to let him down. However, as Dyer argues, the ideas of whiteness, to be nothing, to be invisible is unattainable, a fact that Warhol reluctantly acknowledges: "Day after day I look in the mirror and I still see something – a new pimple."[21] The double that Warhol feared was not a representation of himself (which he found liberating; either in the form of idealised portraits or Alan Midgette acting as a stand-in) but the corporeal original. Try as he might he could never escape this fleshly double, it always returned to haunt him, whether in the form of a pimple or a bullet.

Warhol dealt with many of the fears of the white man (of being death/ dead, being non-reproductive, being nothing) not simply by facing them head on, but by attempting to absorb and assimilate them within himself. This makes him unusual in the history of white masculinity as the general trend has been to externalise rather than internalise such fears. These external manifestations have taken many forms from Moby Dick, and Dracula to more contemporary examples such as the androids in the films of Ridley Scott. The android, while a manifest fear (like the homosexual and the vampire it too is unable to reproduce), is also an aspirational figure as it represents purity and absence of affect; it is the observing subject without properties. I have suggested that Warhol shared this aspiration and that his oft-quoted claim that he wanted to be a machine suggests as much. His assertion that the acquisition of his tape recorder finished off his (already attenuated) emotional life would also seem to point to his aspiration to be machine-like. The fact that Warhol seemed prepared to deny his humanity (his subjectivity) and embrace what are seen as the unattractive, fearsome attributes of the machine is often what unnerves his detractors. He is portrayed, in the words of Philip K. Dick, the creator of Scott's androids, as "the machine, lacking empathy, watching as mere spectator [...] [the] figure which sees but gives no assistance, offers no hand."[22] However, as I have suggested, Warhol's cold, robotic exterior is perhaps not representative of his interior but a prosthesis, a mask, to protect it. Dick again:

> ... the true face is the reverse of the mask. Of course it would be. You do not place fierce cold metal over fierce cold metal. You place it over soft flesh, as the harmless moth adorns itself artfully to terrorise others with ocilli. This is a defensive measure.[23]

Whilst becoming an object has, as Warhol shows, the positive advantage of offering the soft subject a protective shell, it also extracts a price that is higher than most are prepared to pay. While attaining the pinnacle of whiteness, the subject without properties, can offer "an ecstasy to be felt in [...] luminescent representation [...], a luminescence that makes sense in the context of whiteness as transcendence, dissolution [...] and no-thing-ness,"[24] within this ecstasy lurks an anxiety "the desolate suspicion of non-existence."[25] This anxiety is perhaps well founded and its basis is fluently expressed in both Warhol's work and image. Both Warhol and Monroe reached such a peak of cultural construction that, to an extent, it ceases to be relevant whether these constructions emerged from 'real' people. This anxiety is demonstrated in the public's desperate need to construct subjects from the empty images of stars, hence the many, often prurient and intrusive, biographies of Marilyn, Diana, Elvis et al. Monroe perhaps shared such an anxiety and this may explain her reluctance to entirely separate her subject and object. On the face of it Warhol harboured no such anxieties, he seemed prepared to dissolve into his images, to mediate all his actions and interactions with machinery in order to become more machine-like, to accept the death of his subjectivity with equanimity. However, the screen that he constructed around himself was tough but not bullet proof. After the shooting he put himself back together and claimed that more than ever before he felt that he was watching television rather than living life, but the chinks in his armour were beginning to be visible to those who cared to look hard enough. When Baby Jane Holzer said that she thought that since the shooting, Andy was one of the happiest people she knew, Sam Green snapped back, "He's as badly off as Marilyn Monroe."[26]

In his later years, Warhol also exhibited the characteristics of another model of white male identity – the body-builder. This seems an unlikely role for a famously effete and fragile artist, but a photograph from 1982 shows him working out in a gym, lifting weights and displaying an impressive set of biceps. The statuesque white torso was a familiar image to Warhol as a voracious consumer of gay pornography and muscle magazines (which he maintained were one and the same); but it was only after he was shot that he aspired to become such. No doubt this stemmed partly from a practical desire to improve his physical strength, but may also have offered him psychological comfort. Dyer writes:

> ... a hard, contoured body does not look like it runs the risk of being merged into other bodies. A sense of separation and boundedness is important to the white male ego. [...] a model of white male identity and survival of the self are expressed through fantasmic fears of the flooding, invading character of women, the masses and racial inferiors. Only a hard, visibly bounded body can resist being submerged into the horror of femininity and non-whiteness.[27]

Viva, one of Warhol's 'superstars' and at one time a close friend, maintained that after the assassination attempt by Valerie Solanis he became genuinely terrified of women and that his already strong aversion to physical contact increased: "He was sexually afraid of women before, I mean you couldn't touch him, he would cringe. That could have been an act, but afterwards he seemed deeply afraid."[28] After one woman had managed to penetrate his screen of objectivity and invade his person, he was not prepared to run the risk of a reoccurrence and hardened both mind and body accordingly.

The picture that I have painted of Warhol implies an interesting contradiction. He is generally positioned within art history as the first genuinely postmodern artist, symbolic of a paradigm shift. This is largely an accurate assessment; he catapulted popular culture and mass media techniques into the fine art canon, embraced commodity culture, was the very embodiment of the 'hyperreal' and abandoned universal truths in favour of everyday banalities. However, his aspiration to culturally white undermines the certainty of this position. To be the highest point of the Enlightenment's intellectual ideal, the observing subject without properties – an object – is surely a Modernist ambition. Likewise his artwork; for all its apparent dissimilarities with Modern art, shares with it an aim to cast an objective eye over the human condition. This ambiguity on Warhol's part can perhaps be attributed, like Monroe's, to his historical position. They were both figures 'on the cusp', signifying, like Warhol's portraits and the movie screen, a process of death and rebirth, the transition from one era to another with, perversely, Monroe representing a death and Warhol, a new life.

NOTES

1 Richard Dyer, *White*, Routledge, London, 1997, p. 209.

2 Ibid., p. 210.

3 Victor Bockris, *Warhol*, Penguin, London, 1989, 1990 edition, p. 236.

4 Judith Halberstam, *Skin Shows: Gothic Horror and the Technology of Monsters*, Duke University Press, Durham & London, 1995, p. 88.

5 Bockris, op cit., p. 411.

6 Jonathan Flatley, "Warhol Gives Good Face: Publicity and the Politics of Prosopopeia", in *PopOut: Queer Warhol* ed. by Jennifer Doyle, Jonathan Flatley & Jose Esteban Munoz, Duke University Press, Durham & London, 1996, p. 107.

7 Ibid., p. 107.

8 Ibid., p. 105.

9 Kirk Varnedoe, Chief Curator, Department of Painting and Sculpture, MoMA, New York, quoted in Robert Hughes' *American Visions*, BBC2, 22 December 1996.

10 Flatley, op cit., p. 106.

11 Ibid., p. 107.

12 Ibid., p. 113.

13 Bockris, op cit., p. 230.

14 Grant McCracken, *Big Hair: A Journey into the Transformation of Self*, Indigo, London, 1997, p. 97.

15 Ibid., p. 92.

16 Daniel Herwitz, *Making Theory/ Constructing Art: On the Authority of the Avant-Garde*, University of Chicago, London, 1993, 1995 edition, p. 243.

17 Flatley, op cit., p. 113.

18 Andy Warhol, *From A to B and Back Again: The Philosophy of Andy Warhol*, Picador, London, 1976, 1979 edition, p. 83.

19 Jean Baudrillard, *Symbolic Exchange and Death*, Sage, London, 1993, p. 142.

20 Steven Shaviro, "Warhol before the mirror" in, *Who is Andy Warhol?*, ed. by Colin MacCabe, Mark Francis & Peter Woollen, BFI, London, 1997, p. 89.

21 Ibid., p. 90.

22 Philip K. Dick, "Man, Android and Machine" in *Science Fiction at Large: A Collection of Essays, by Various Hands, about the Interface between Science Fiction and Reality*, ed. by Peter Nicholls, Victor Gollancz, London, 1976, p. 218.

23 Ibid., p. 204.

24 Dyer, op cit., p. 80.

25 Ibid., p. 45.

26 Bockris, op cit., p. 391.

27 Dyer, op cit., pp. 152-153.

28 Bockris, op cit., p. 379.

GROPING IN THE DARK

ENCOUNTERING THE WORKS OF STEVE MCQUEEN

DIANA YEH

At the beginning of 1999, Steve McQueen had his first solo exhibition in the UK. Later that year he won the Turner Prize. The following essay, written at the time of the solo exhibition at the ICA (30 January-21 March 1999), reviews McQueen's early works and anticipates his present acclaim but questions its critical reception.

In his essay, "Haptic Visions: The Films of Steve McQueen",[1] Okwui Enwezor isolates a comment on *Deadpan* (1997) written by a *New York Times* reviewer, following an exhibition at the Museum of Modern Art in New York:

> Seen in an American context, the house suggests a sharecropper's cabin; its destruction evokes Abraham Lincoln's Civil War caveat, 'a house divided against itself cannot stand,' referring to a nation riven by the question of slavery. (Mr McQueen is black.)[2]

Enwezor responds,

> Enough. The critic in question does the most incongruous thing, by
> shifting radically from the proper reading of the film, to questions of
> race, which are not even remotely connected to the artist's intention.

This dispute neatly encapsulates two crudely categorised and generally
opposed theoretical positions in art criticism, identified by Raymond
Williams as the 'formalist' and the 'sociological', which have reappeared in
discussions of Steve McQueen's works.[3] The formalist stance adopted by
Enwezor stresses the necessity of attending to the specific properties of a
work, while the sociological tends toward the appropriation of a work in
terms of its presumed social content. That this divide has resurfaced in
response to McQueen's works is hardly surprising, given the highly
sensitive terrain of the critical assessment of art by non-white artists.

As Enwezor concedes, the 'absurd' reading of *Deadpan* results from the
way in which the black figure functions as a political image in
contemporary culture. The marginality of black arts has structurally
determined its development, conferring upon artists the 'burden of
representation'.[4] As Richard Dyer explains, "there is no more powerful
position than that of being 'just' human. The claim to power is the claim
to speak for the communality of humanity. Raced people can't do that –
they can only speak for their race."[5] If this is the case, then a seemingly
peculiar thing has occurred in the discourse accompanying McQueen's
ICA exhibition. Art critics and curators have provided purely formal
assessments of the artist's work, avoiding all reference to his ethnic origin.
Undoubtedly, this may signify a positive critical move away from previous
sociological approaches that have contributed to the ghettoisation of
black arts production. Yet the question is, does the present discourse do
justice to the works by attending exclusively to formal properties or have
critics in fact been blinded by a political correctness that prevents them
from acknowledging an important facet of McQueen's works?

Following Stuart Hall we may ask, "What sort of moment is this to
pose the question?" I would argue that the 'whitening' of McQueen's

work is the product of a specific historical moment of the late nineties, where the production of black art and its critical reception are operating from a position informed by past 'mistakes'. Just four years before, responding to another ICA exhibition *Mirage – Enigmas of Race, Difference and Desire*, critics happily assessed McQueen's work along racial lines. Perhaps his earlier works, *Bear* (1993), *Five Easy Pieces* (1995) and *Just Above My Head* (1996), absent from his exhibition, are more susceptible to 'sociological' readings. The subjects of these films are black and, as Raimi Gbadamosi suggests, "where the self is a 'canvas of representation', and the black body is already politicised by the history it carries, art merely has to point to a black person, or a black person's concern to become political."[6] Such readings were legitimised – even encouraged – by the framing of the exhibition around Frantz Fanon's *Black Skin White Masks*. The institutionalised rhetoric of postcolonialism that proffers such exhibitions renders cultural products more docile and 'theorizable'. "The exotic other that once invited territorial/physical exploration now invites as well as justifies theoretical exploration."[7] Now, however, in absence of a curatorial framework underpinning McQueen's solo exhibition, difficulties in discussing his work resurface. The reluctance of both black and white critics to explore potentially political implications of McQueen's work may stem from the very fear of ghettoising him as a black artist. As Gilroy suggests, "a commitment to the mystique of cultural insiderism and the myths of cultural homogeneity [...] is directly related to a dangerous variety of political timidity that culminates in a reluctance to debate some racial subjects because they are too sensitive to be aired."[8]

In this review, therefore, I attempt to walk the "tightrope between the Scylla of reductionism and the Charybdis of aestheticism"[9] to reveal aspects of McQueen's works that have been ignored in the arguably hegemonic formalist approaches. By locating artist and artworks in the framework of black cultural politics as defined by Stuart Hall in "New Ethnicities",[10] I suggest that McQueen's works are in dialogue with, but ultimately transcend former strategies of black representation. At first sight, his later works – *White Elephant* (1998), *Drumroll* (1998), *Barrage* (1998) and *Untitled* (1999) – appear to mark a shift in concerns and conceptual problems from his earlier films – *Bear* (1993), *Five Easy Pieces* (1995), *Just Above My Head* (1996) and *Deadpan* (1997). This shift seems to coincide with the two stages of black cultural politics defined by Hall as a move from the confirmation of an essential fixed black identity in the 'relations of representation' to that of an unstable, dispersed and fragmented identity in the 'politics of representation'. McQueen's works however, are not merely representative of the two moments. In choosing to reject or embrace elements of both, McQueen displays a firm comprehension of the precedents involved, retaining only strategies that remain useful and abandoning those that, in today's climate of supposed multiculturalism, have become redundant.

The discrepancy between McQueen's works and earlier black strategies are partly explained in terms of intended audiences. While many black artists, including those of the BLK Art movement,[11] declared that their work addressed a black public, McQueen is entering a predominantly 'white' art world and must therefore remain aware of the politics involved in the reception of black arts. As Robert Storr suggests,

> ... while McQueen is determined to show us something for its own sake, he is always mindful that who does the showing is a part of the content that is finally absorbed by the viewer. 'No' in theory, an experimental artist's colour should not matter, but 'Yes', when the experiment is run in public space, it does. And so McQueen takes note of himself, and of his voice, and of patterns of response as he makes his way.[12]

Thus, while first examining McQueen's works in the light of former black cultural strategies, I also illustrate that his work aims specifically to problematise critical reception. In fact, it is perhaps McQueen's ingenuity on this account that has led to the crisis in reception of his work, causing critics to seek refuge in either the formalist or socio-political camp. To return to Enwezor, what *would* constitute a 'proper' reading of his work? The problem inherent in sociological readings applies equally to the formalist approach advocated by Enwezor – namely, the artificial separation of 'form' and 'content'. McQueen's works demand a reading in which these are seen not only as inextricably entwined, but continually operating in synchronisation and opposition to one another. The fundamental value of the final artwork lies in the very tension between the two.

McQueen's Modernist aesthetics undoubtedly encourages formalist readings. Drawing almost exclusively on European art film traditions, he produces formally strict and visually grand film shorts that insistently evoke both film and art history. Critics point to influences from Eisenstein, Dreyer and Bresson, to Rodchenko, Caravaggio, Decavara, to Warhol and Nauman. While not denying these influences, their overemphasis appears to insist "that Modernist aesthetics are naturally 'colour-blind' and that theorizing the specificity of race is therefore unnecessary."[13] Since black artists previously united in a search for a 'black aesthetic' to revitalise black art against the "bankrupt aestheticism of Western Modernism",[14] Modernism for black artists has been viewed as an indulgence or evasion of social responsibilities. With hindsight however, it is evident that the prescriptive demands of the black aesthetic have bound the black artist ever more closely to his burden.[15] McQueen's works demand an examination of political implications inherent in the artistic choices at the level of film form as he works through issues of race (amongst others) at a formal level. As Michael Newman suggests, McQueen "does not content himself with appropriation or stereotype, he rather directs attention to the refunctioning of form."[16]

The tendency to avoid reference to McQueen's ethnicity has been fuelled by his public persona. Unlike the declared political activism of many black artists,[17] McQueen refrains from discussing racial politics: "I want people to think beyond race, nationality and all that kind of crap... This debate is tired, ugly and beat-up."[18] His refusal to be categorised as a black artist with specific social responsibilities appears less as a disinterest in, or abdication of racial issues, than a necessary stance adopted to prevent political issues presiding over artistic concerns. Given that "any possible label or affiliation is used to point out difference'[9] McQueen's comment "I don't deal with Black and White"[20] seems an attempt to redress the over-politicised nature of black artists today. McQueen is first an artist, and then he is also black.

This set of priorities is revealed in his work. While in the eighties, 'blackness' and by extension 'black art' referred to the common experience of racism, McQueen's works explore a 'human' experience. His subjects, rather than just 'being black', are engaged with dedication in self-imposed tasks, whether tight-rope walking, wrestling, withstanding the collapse of a house, rolling an oil-drum, or simply walking. This immediately invalidates race-relations discourse in which blacks become visible only as problems of society or victims of racial oppression. McQueen presents individuals marked by a confident self-possession, vulnerable only to the challenges they have set themselves. Even in *Exodus* (1992/1997) which recalls the history of slavery and subsequent enforced migrations, the subjects are impervious to any supposed 'victimisation'. The film records a real event filmed on the fly, and captures two West Indian men near Brick Lane carrying palm trees and boarding a bus. Diaspora experience is presented humorously as the plants sway majestically and the two smiling men wave happily to the camera as if conscious of the irony of their return to the promised homeland of Wood Green.

McQueen follows his predecessors in excavating past representations of blacks in dominant discourse, yet with greater subtlety and complexity. Eddie Chambers, for example, explored stereotypes in overtly confrontational works such as *The Black Bastard as a Cultural Icon*, making collages with photographs extracted from newspapers and ethnographic journals to demonstrate the culturally in-built nature of racism. McQueen, however, adopts the 'invitational' mode, making the viewer become aware of his own unconscious prejudices. As he has said "I want to put people in a situation where they're sensitive to themselves watching the piece."[21]

His films are interlaced with images, which, decontextualised from the realm of racial discourse, strike the unprepared viewer by revealing the workings of his unconscious associations. In *Deadpan*, for example, while our attention is focused on the impending collapse of the house, we see portrait shots of McQueen head-on and in profile. The viewer immediately recognises these familiar images as stereotyped snapshots of the 'black man as criminal',[22] yet since they function in the film to map out our different perspectives on the event, we are made aware that the association comes from our own *musée imaginaire* of black culture.

A similar technique is used in *Bear*. Located in the middle of the film is the interjection of a close-up of a man's head, motionless and framed like a skull on a pedestal. The slowing of the film speed, the introduction of colour and the grainy texture of the film create a marked change in atmosphere. By foregrounding the medium, McQueen interrupts the ideological purpose of naturalistic illusion. The fluid dream-like quality of the camera motion appeals to the viewer on an unconscious level, to his 'optical unconscious'.[23] The camera navigates the man's facial topography, studying the nose, the lips and the eyes in turn with an enquiring ethnographic gaze. Then, almost imperceptibly, the camera collides with the object of the gaze to become an eye looking out at the viewer, who suddenly realises that he is being watched by the camera, through the gaze of the man's eyes. Subject and object are reversed, and the discomfort of being the viewer is relieved only by the humiliation of becoming the viewed.

Play with the duration and movement of film is used extensively and oscillates between the apparent slowing down of film speed at moments of high tension, and the resuming of pace in narrative. During the slow build-up of each climactic moment, a space is hollowed out inviting the viewer to examine his responses to the imagery and his expectations of narrative denouement, before both are confounded and the tension is released. Form is used to interrogate content, in this case, the two dominant stereotypical fears of black masculinity, namely sexuality and

45

violence. As the title *Bear* suggests, McQueen takes on "the burden of being perceived through [...] the already-read text of debasedness and animality."[24] The nakedness of the men simultaneously suggests and empties the potency of black male sexuality. At first, the camera lingers suffocatingly close to the subjects creating sensual images of the sweat and texture of skin, reminiscent of Mapplethorpe's controversial photographs of black nudes. As the cinematic eye becomes fixated on the black bodies, again, a temporal space is created which invites viewers to question their reactions to such images and "whose fantasies, specifically, are allowed on [...] the public screen."[25] McQueen thus enacts Kobena Mercer's challenge to the notion that the pleasure derived from Mapplethorpe's photographs necessarily implicates the viewer in an act of dehumanisation. In taking control of the erotic representation of the black male nude from dominant discourse, McQueen simultaneously confirms and mocks our dependency on the knowledge of his racial background and the notion of 'ethnic insiderism' that legitimise his portrayals.

Having built up a powerful eroticism, the potency of 'black male sexuality' is then undercut by a move from the narrow focus of fetishistic voyeurism to the development of a narrative that charts the shifting emotional and physical relationship of two wrestlers. McQueen has said, "the body in art, the body in film and video, the body, the body... It reduces things. It is not just the body." Indeed the two 'decidedly anti-Mapplethorpean black men'[26] are not confined to just 'being' their bodies; they are engaged in mock battle. As they lock in an inconclusive struggle, a shot from below presents the vulnerability of their genitalia. The black male body, McQueen shows, has nothing to signify. As the camera attends closely to every shift in facial and bodily expression, the film becomes less a study of black male sexuality than an exploration of human emotion. The theme of violence is undercut by a narrative move into the playful cuffing between the men, which develops into a flirtation reminiscent of a mating ritual where the more effeminate of the two teases the other provocatively. The relationship verges on the transformation into a homoerotic encounter, before this too is dispelled into tenderness, and an affectionate, brotherly embrace.

In changing the relations of representation, black artists have also struggled against exclusion from the mainstream arts. *Just Above My Head,* which references James Baldwin's 1979 novel,[27] has often been interpreted as a statement on marginalisation; "the visibility of the black artist, his place both at the centre and margins of things."[28] The camera tracks a vast expanse of white cloudy sky against which the artist's head is seen bobbing along at the bottom of the frame. As McQueen's pace quickens or slows, the frame includes and excludes more of him. This continues in an almost unbearable monotony, until suddenly "an electrifying epiphanic moment"[29] occurs when the branches of a tree break the frame and sprawl across the screen. In terms of content, rather than a comment on marginalisation, *Just Above My Head* is a poignant presentation of meditation, of the vastness of all that is ungraspable, and about the sudden dawning of an understanding that, in the end, still changes nothing at all.

The theme of marginalisation arises but on a purely formal level of interrogating blackness and whiteness as filmic qualities.[30] The black head thrown against a white sky brings to mind Zola Neale Hurston's comment "I feel most coloured when I am thrown against a sharp white background." McQueen's work thus recalls that figure-ground relations have been developed according to the norm of white skin and draws attention to the exclusions involved in the formal history of the medium of film. While "photographing non-white people is typically construed as a problem",[31] the fact is that film technology was developed to privilege white skin over black. In this light, particularly in *Bear* and *Five Easy Pieces,* McQueen demonstrates how one can use lighting to depict black skin. The blackness presented is undefined by whiteness, or rather, contains whiteness within itself. The bodies oscillate between black and white according to the structural necessity of the works. In *Bear,* the wrestlers' legs appear white, the details of their muscles and tendons recalling Greco-Roman statues. Similarly, in *Five Easy Pieces*, the woman's back is strongly lit and produces a white plane that splits the frame diagonally against the black background. As Michael Newman states, McQueen "gives a hint of what cinema might have been had it included black subjects as central to its project."[32]

'Black art' is still marginalised but as it becomes increasingly centred, traditional structures of national identity are becoming ever more fractured. As Stuart Hall has said, "Now that, in the postmodern age, you all feel so dispersed, I become centred. What I've thought of as dispersed and fragmented comes, paradoxically, to be *the* representative modern experience."[33] McQueen's post-1998 works coincide with this shift from the presentation of identity as fixed and stable to one that is unstable, fragmented and dispersed. Yet the question arises, "whose identity?" McQueen does embrace the notion of an unstable identity, but it belongs not to him but to the viewer of his work. Nowhere is this more explicit than in *White Elephant* (1998), an installation of the drum of a Praxinoscope enlarged into a mirrored chrome roundabout. As we walk around or sit on it, we become conscious that our presence is being continually obliterated. At best our bodies are reflected as fragments and unless we lean vertiginously over the work, it is easy to see nothing but the surrounding garish pink walls. If we spin on the roundabout, the experience created by the harsh lighting reflecting the shriekingly pink walls literally induces a physical nausea. As with many of McQueen's works, a play on gravity is central to *White Elephant*. The nearer to the centre one is, the less unsettled one would feel, but McQueen has blocked out this possibility by the central placing of a heavy chrome ball.

This disorientating experience is continued in *Drumroll*, a triptych projecting images of three different perspectives of a Manhattan street, recorded by installing three cameras in an oil-drum that is rolled down the street. The title heralds the event of McQueen, the migrant in the metropolis, taking the post-colonial city by storm. As he strolls with determination, clearing the crowd obstructing his way by the occasional "Excuse me... Sorry" the viewer struggles to maintain his balance as his senses are thrown into frenzy. The work stands out in the use of both colour and sound, with the real time recording of the cacophony of chaotic city life and the kaleidoscopic vision of street colours. As with David Hammon's *Phat Free* (1995–1997), this work speaks of "urban nomadism, of marginal geographies and migrations, and indirectly but unmistakably, of the bittersweet 'liberties' of African-American life."[34] Just as black slaves of the past transformed their steel drums into musical instruments for creative expression, so McQueen takes on the job of creating a "formally cohesive and vividly Simultaneist vision of the modern city."[35] The piece echoes the traditions of black music with its use of improvisation and antiphony – both are articulated in an aesthetic of performance, asserting a priority of expression over artefact.

Seen in this light, it is possible to trace a connection between McQueen's earlier and later works. While the black and white films disturb the viewer by inviting reactions to racial imagery, the subsequent works force the viewer to acknowledge his own unstable identity. As I suggested earlier, McQueen's works span not only the two phases in black cultural politics, but challenge critical reception as well by creating a problematic relationship between viewer and medium. For each of his films, McQueen specifies the viewing conditions necessary to create a reciprocal and mutually interpolated relationship between the art and the audience. The 'films' are rather installations, images projected from the floor to the ceiling and wall to wall, such that the viewer is physically subsumed into the work. McQueen thus renders the gallery space "a zone that is simultaneously haptic and optical."[36] In *Deadpan*, for example, the black cube of the installation induces a feeling of spatial dislocation. As the house collapses, McQueen stands stock-still, while debris, earth and dust fly out onto the viewer, creating a suffocating experience.

McQueen also uses shots that place the viewer in a submissive position in relation to image. This is particularly evident in *Five Easy Pieces* where abrupt positional cutting is foregrounded, oscillating between images of grace and irreverence. First the viewer looks up at the tense and still tightrope walker, then down to an aerial shot of the twirling hula-hoopers. "One minute we are flying like birds, the next we are debased and crawling on our bellies."[37] Our eyes again strain upward only to be met by a close-up of a man's crotch as he gyrates in an overtly sexual manner. This image transmutes into a similar shot from below of McQueen standing in his boxer shorts. Taking his penis from his shorts, he urinates and then spits – one imagines – on any attempt to impose a clear reading on his works whether in terms of theory or aesthetics. The impudence of the content and the beauty of the form simultaneously shocks and placates the viewer who is momentarily stunned by contradictory responses. First we are insulted at being blinded by urine, then enchanted by the visual beauty of the bubbling liquid, and finally humoured by McQueen's audacity and the fact that somehow we end up grateful that he has pissed on us. In this work, and all others, McQueen represents the stable identity in perfect control, while we, his victims, are fragmented by our conflicting aesthetic, social and political responses.

McQueen's concern with the relationship between the viewer and the artwork extends to an awareness of the interactions between these and the gallery space. I have already mentioned the artist's precise specifications for his installations, fundamental to their full appreciation. McQueen's works, however, draw our attention not only to our aesthetic experience but to an awareness of the "situations, the occasions, the signals which release that response."[38] The white space of the gallery is transformed by the construction of black and pink cubes, which function both as the exhibition space and an intrinsic part of each work. In contrast to other works, with *Untitled* (1999), a brick wall constructed along the ICA's concourse, art becomes artefact and the aesthetic is only released by the situation of the observer and the placing of the object. We thus become aware of the gallery space as a constructed environment, and the violence of the broken glass embedded in the wall leads us to question the power structures employed in constructing an exhibition. The fact that the brick wall has been erected solely for the exhibition guarantees its future demolition and so draws our attention to the specificity of the historical moment in which we encounter McQueen's works. While this work highlights the present moment, *White Elephant* is an excavation of the past and the history of cinema. As the title suggests, the work can be seen as the burden of history where present (black or other) modes of creative expression must negotiate former strategies of representation.

In analysing McQueen's work, it seems I have come full circle. The questions I have raised seem to have been pre-empted by McQueen's works. At the beginning of the essay, I suggested that the 'either/or' dichotomy of the formalistic/sociological readings of McQueen's works were inadequate. In an attempt to redress the balance of current criticism, I have examined McQueen's work in the framework of black cultural production while paying attention to the political implications of his work on a formal level. As I have shown, his works not only span the two moments from the relations of representation to the politics of representation, but also far exceed them by reclaiming the aesthetic quality of blackness and whiteness from politics. Yet, it is not only the boundaries of black cultural representation that he breaks. His works reveal a concern for the very dichotomy of the formalist and sociological categories by provoking a confrontation between the two. Even more, he breaks down the traditional separation of the arts into generic categories by producing works that are at once sculptural, photographic, filmic and painterly and that transform our experience of the art gallery itself.

In focusing on the relationship between the viewer and his works, in such a way that the viewer is continually questioned, confounded and disorientated, McQueen reveals the need for a revision of critical theory if we are to keep up with artists as complex and sophisticated as he. Yet it seems that any analysis, whether emphasising the formal or socio-political elements of his works, must remain provisional. McQueen's multi-faceted works make it almost impossible to provide any definitive reading. While providing us with fodder for intellectual debates on a host of issues, he offers no directives that would suggest a conclusive statement. Perhaps a more adequate model of criticism may be derived from the critical practice performed in the artworks themselves. The physicality of his art requires that "primary emotional reaction is the predicate for critical response."[39] In a culture based on excess, where conflicting sights, odours and sounds of modern urban life bombard our senses, McQueen's works force us to recover our senses, and see, hear, and feel, while confounding our intellectual interpretations. His distaste for presupposed critical discourse around his work accentuates the inherently problematic relationship between art and theory, and returns us to the need for an 'erotics of art'. McQueen thus succeeds in eluding interpreters "by making works of art whose surface is unified and clean, whose momentum is so rapid, whose address is so direct that the work can be... just what it is."[40]

Yet while wholeheartedly embracing McQueen's works, one must return to the problem that initially sparked this investigation, namely the whitewashing of McQueen within the art world. We may celebrate his success, but remain wary of the reception that has enabled his success. The worry is that he may function as a token within institutions that are unwilling to acknowledge the real challenges that lie in his work. It is too early to jump to any conclusions, so, as with all his works, we must wait and watch his moves.

NOTES

1 Okwui Enwezor, Haptic Visions: The Films of Steve McQueen', in *Steve McQueen*, ICA catalogue, ICA in collaboration with the Kunsthalle Zurich, London, 1999, pp. 35-48.

2 Ibid. p. 47.

3 Raymond Williams, *Politics and Letters: Interviews with 'New Left Review'*, NLB, London, 1979.

4 Kobena Mercer, *Welcome to the Jungle: New Positions in Black Cultural Studies*, Routledge, London, 1994.

5 Richard Dyer, *White*, Routledge, London, 1997, p. 2.

6 Raimi Gbadamosi, "Am I Black Enough?", *Third Text*, 44, 1998, pp. 69-78, p. 70.

7 Saeed Ur-Rehman, "Decolonizing Post-Colonial Theory", *Kunapipi Journal of Post Colonial Writing*, 20, 1998, 31-39, p. 33.

8 Paul Gilroy, *Small Facts – Thoughts on the Politics of Black Cultures*, Serpent's Tail, London & New York, 1993, p. 101.

9 Cornel West, "The New Cultural Politics of Difference" in *The Cultural Studies Reader*, ed. by Simon During, Routledge, London & New York, 1993, pp. 203–217, p. 214.

10 Stuart Hall, "New Ethnicities" in *Black Film, British Cinema*, ed. by Kobena Mercer and others,. ICA Documents No. 7, 1988, pp. 27-31.

11 Artists such as Eddie Chambers and Keith Piper set up the BLK Art movement to support and promote art by black artists. See also note 17.

12 Robert Storr, "Going Places" in *Steve McQueen*, ICA catalogue, ICA in collaboration with Kunsthalle Zurich, London, 1999, pp. 7-18, p. 16.

13 Coco Fusco, "The Other Is In: Black British Film in the US" in *Black Film, British Cinema*, ed. by Kobena Mercer and others, ICA Documents No. 7, 1988, pp. 37-39, p. 38.

14 Mercer, p. 15.

15 Paul Gilroy's studies have since suggested that the cross-cultural 'cut and mix' of styles is fundamental to diasporic culture. See Paul Gilroy, *The Black Atlantic: Modernity and the Double Consciousness*, Verso, London, 1993.

16 Michael Newman, "McQueen's Materialism" in *Steve McQueen*, ICA catalogue, ICA in collaboration with Kunsthalle Zurich, London, 1999, pp. 21-35, p. 22.

17 During the eighties, an era of political certainty, Eddie Chambers

53

of the BLK Art Group described the specific function of Black Art: "It should seek to effect [...] change by aiming to help us create an alternative set of values necessary to better living. Otherwise it fails to be legitimate art." Quoted in Rasheed Araeen's *The Other Story: Afro-Asian Artists in Post-War Britain,* South Bank Centre, London, 1989, pp. 72-73.

18 Iwona Blazwick, "Oh my God!" *make– the magazine of women's art,* 74, 1997, pp. 5-7, p. 6.

19 Gbdamosi, p. 77.

20 Patricia Bickers, "Let's Get Physical: Steve McQueen interviewed by Patricia Bickers", *Art Monthly,* 202, 1996–1997, pp. 1-5, p. 4. McQueen says in the same interview, "Obviously being black is a part of me... I just want to make work. People try to contain things by putting them into categories. I don't."

21 Ibid. p. 2.

22 See also Keith Piper's *Mapping the Face – Adventures Close to Home,* 1992.

23 Walter Benjamin's term discussed in Rosalind Krauss, *The Optical Unconscious,* The MIT Press, Cambridge & Massachusetts, 1993.

24 Henry Louis Gates Jr., as quoted in Martha Gever's "Steve McQueen" in *Spellbound: Art and Film,* Hayward Gallery & BFI, London, 1996, pp. 93-99, p. 95.

25 Ibid. p. 98.

26 Christian Haye, "Motion Pictures: Christian Haye on Steve McQueen", *Frieze,* 28, 1996, pp. 40-43, p .42.

27 James Baldwin, *Just Above My Head,* Joseph, London, 1979.

28 Adrian Searle, "The Good, The Bad, The Ugly", *The Guardian,* 8 October 1996.

29 Jon Thompson, "'It's the Way You Tell 'Em': Narrative Cliché in the Films of Steve McQueen" in *Steve McQueen,* Portikus, Frankfurt am-Main, Stedelijk Van Abbemuseum, Eindhoven, 1997, pp. 5-9, p. 9.

30 Interest in 'whiteness' extends back to James Baldwin and Ralph Ellison but has recently seen a renaissance with Toni Morrison's *Playing in the Dark: Whiteness and the Literary Imagination*, and Cornel West's call for an explanation of the ways in which 'whiteness' is a politically constructed category parasitic on 'blackness'.

31 Dyer, p. 89.

32 Newman, p. 24.

33 Hall, p. 44.

34 Storr, p. 16.

35 Ibid. p. 16.

36 Enwezor, p. 36.

37 Thompson, p. 7.

38 Williams, 1979.

39 Storr, p. 14.

40 Susan Sontag, "Against Interpretation" in *The Philosophy of Art: Readings Ancient and Modern*, ed. by Alex Neill and Aaron Ridley, pp. 457-465, p. 463.

WHITENESS

Richard Dyer remarks in his book, *White*, "Few things have delighted the
white press as much as the disfigurement of Michael Jackson's face
through what have been supposed to be his attempts to become white."[1]
The sentence begs three questions. Firstly, are we to read the qualified
"supposed... attempts" as a latent doubt about the real objective of
Jackson's transformation? Secondly, by naming the press as 'white' are we
meant to construe the whiteness that Jackson seeks in racial terms only?
And, lastly, should the pejorative term 'disfigurement' be accepted? It does
seem that Dyer has left room to question the assumptions the press has
made about Jackson's decades-long whiteness project. But, just as Dyer
opens that door, he seems to close another.

Were these much-chronicled surgeries undertaken at vast expense only to arrive at a disfigured face? Could *The Guinness Book of World Records'* best-selling music artist of all time, the plotting businessman who bought the rights tö the Beatles catalogue out from under Sir Paul McCartney, be out to purposefully disfigure his face in a foiled attempt to pass as white? Can Michael Jackson's face be read in terms other than race? If his face is not about racial trans-formation, can it be viewed as something other than mere disfigurement?

PASSING INTEREST

The 'tragic mulatto' is a film character type Donald Bogle locates in a clutch of films from 1912-1913 and later again with the work of certain actresses from the thirties and forties. Fredi Washington is described by the press "as looking French or Italian".[2] Lena Horne unintentionally sparked controversy with her first film appearance. "MGM received a number of letters from whites asking who their new Latin American discovery was. At the same time, MGM was accused by some irate Negroes of attempting to pass her off as white."[3] Passing and show business are especially linked for Bogle, who reads the genre as a film subject and then as a theme peripheral to film itself, but known to the audience through the press. An inverse condition of passing is outlined in Bogle's critique of D.W. Griffith's *The Birth of a Nation* where "white actors in blackface" play black roles. This is not to be confused with the blackface of Minstrelsy. Vaudeville acts like Al Jolson were never intended to pass white for black, but were consciously stylised. "The minstrel visage – broad whitened lips in a blackened face, the caricature of a caricature –

Al Jolson, *The Singing Kid*
1936

has become the most enduring of black caricatures. It has inspired another enduring entertainment figure: the clown type of 'dummer August', modelled on the minstrel."[4] It is important to note that this face is not in any way a realistic depiction, but a theatrical device. The performance of minstrel actors was given "license all the greater because it took place behind black masks."[5]

MOTOWN

The Jackson 5 had been playing small venues from the time Michael was seven years old. After producer Berry Gordy signed the act with Motown Records, the group was introduced to television audiences by Diana Ross who was said to have 'discovered' Michael and his brothers. Much has been made of the friendship shared by the former Supreme and the child star, not the least of which is the charge that Jackson would later in adulthood model his face on her's. But this correspondence is not borne out by comparing their actual faces. Perhaps, the popular analogy is a way of pointing out the sexual neutrality of Jackson's face, or even its perceived femininity. Lacan, rejecting Freud's narrow definitions for masculine and feminine ideals, introduces the term 'masquerade':

> Masquerade is not that which comes into play in the display necessary, at the level of animals, to coupling, and in any case display is usually to be seen on the side of the male. Masquerade has another meaning in the human domain, and that is precisely to play not at the imaginary, but at the symbolic, level.[6]

Motown as charm school determined the appearance of its artists, even their manners. Ross and Jackson were amongst the best students of this system, adopting the Motown 'look' on- and off-stage. While it may be true that male artists were encouraged to de-emphasise overtly masculine, i.e. threatening, elements in their routine, they were never meant to de-emphasise their blackness. The Motown look was never about passing. The very essence of Motown was to push black talent. Even outside of Motown, the heavily made-up black entertainer, from Little Richard to Prince, may have been cited as being sexually ambiguous, but never racially so. Could any artist like Jackson, so inexorably linked to such an institution as Motown ever pretend to pass or even want to pass? What would happen if someone were to emulate black music artists, but refuse to de-emphasise his masculinity?

THE KING OF ROCK

Elvis Presley has been called the first black rock superstar. His assimilation of black music and delivery are legendary. Presley's fame may also stem from the fact that he was free to be explicitly masculine in his performance, to the point that he had to be shot only from the waist up during television appearances for fear of his gyrating hips. Presley dyed his light brown hair black, which can be read as part of his appropriation, but Camille Paglia asserts that Presley's dyed hair tapped into a different tradition altogether. In Michelangelo's *Giuliano de' Medici* sculpture, Paglia finds a new type, different from Graeco-Roman depictions of the androgynous 'beautiful boy'. With *Giuliano*, she locates an "Epicoene, man of beauty."[7] Portraits of Lord Byron represent the Epicoene most clearly. The image is particularly bound up in the contrast between white skin and dark hair.

Jane Porter found Byron's complexion 'softly brilliant', with a 'moonlight paleness'. Lady Blessington called his face 'peculiarly pale', set off by curling hair of 'very dark brown': "He uses a good deal of oil in it, which makes it look still darker." White skin, dark oiled hair: Elvis Presley... despite his friends' urging to let the natural color return. Presley, a myth-maker, understood the essence of his archetypical beauty.[8]
Paglia also comments on the pouting mouths of both Byron and Presley. The curling lip and cleft chin, along with the white skin and dark hair, seem part of the Epicoene face type. There is an implied feminine aspect to the man of beauty, part of the Lacanian masquerade's ability to augment masculinity by incorporating the Other, femininity.

THE KING OF POP

Jackson's publicity machine began referring to him as "the King of Pop" just as he was about to announce his plans for marriage. The appellation, being so akin to Presley's, back-fired in the press, but persisted nonetheless in his press releases and celebrity endorsements. Elizabeth Taylor defends Jackson, calling him "the true King of Pop, Rock and Soul."[9] No one before had dared try to usurp Presley's title. The effort may not have been to replace Elvis, but to co-mingle with his image. To that end, Jackson wed Lisa-Marie Presley and the two spoke of having children some day.

Just as Lisa's mother, Pricilla, had sympathetically dyed her hair black and made-up to complement her husband's famous face, so too did Mrs. Michael Jackson try to become a visual female equivalent of her husband. The result was somewhat less than successful. There simply was little

Photo by the author, Hever Castle, 1999

room for her to feminise an already made-up and stylised face in the tradition of the Epicoene. The daughter of Presley was in fact trying to emulate a face that was already emulating her father's. Despite a celebrated televised kiss and a censored music video showing the couple covorting as naked angels amid Maxfield Parish scenery, the two divorced after two years of marriage.

When Jackson finally did procreate, with his plastic surgeon's nurse, he was quoted by tabloids as being shocked by the fact that the child was utterly white like his mother. Never mind that Jackson's skin was now whiter than either of his wives, he did not seem especially pleased that his offspring should pass for white, rather, he seemed disappointed by it. He named the child Prince; perhaps a pun on Jackson's status as the King of Pop or a reference to one of his competitors who has since become nameless. Jackson is searching for a medieval castle either in the UK or France to house his little Prince.[10] As Jackson and Presley are reported to be seeing each other again, one can imagine their hypothetical child having the choice to winter at Neverland, his father's California ranch-amusement park, summer at Graceland, which his mother will inherit, or stay at the castle. A Jackson-Presley child would stand to inherit the rights to the Elvis, Michael Jackson and Beatles catalogues.

STAGELIGHTS

Jackson has spent all of his adult life and most of his childhood on stage. After signing with Motown as the company's youngest star, his schedule of television performances, interviews and tours with his brothers would proliferate. His subsequent solo career would put the spotlight wholly upon him. Lighting, in general, would become an increasingly important factor in his work as music videos began to dominate the industry. More and more Jackson would need to concern himself not only with his music, but with his image on film. Lighting for the subtleties of dark skin is a technical challenge. Still photographers can control the amount of light hitting celluloid – latitude – to capture more shades of grey or dark colour. Using the 'zone system', one can calculate how much light will hit different areas, spot it and balance it out. Film, on the other hand, cannot be controlled in this way as the intrinsic qualities of film favour lighter surfaces; it is technically partial to light skin. Some current filmmakers, like Julie Dash, have tried to achieve lighting particularly for dark skin compensating for this technicality.

The face of Michael Jackson in the early eighties was consistently saturated with light to render every nuance on film. The lighting became so intense, his hair and make-up caught fire during filming of a Pepsi-Cola commercial. That accident and the subsequent plastic surgery to correct the burns suggested a solution for the film lighting dilemma. Rather than augment the lighting on the face, the face itself might be lightened to Byronesque paleness and so 'balance out' the effect on celluloid.

The marked difference in Jackson's appearance from the album cover of *Thriller* to the next cover for *Bad* reflects the change from before and after the Pepsi-Cola debacle. It must be pointed out that the video for *Thriller* had already introduced Jackson to the world of special effects make-up artists, allowing him to transmogrify from himself to wolf-man to zombie. It is the masculine/feminine polarity described by Freud in Wolf-Man that prompted Lacan to assert the masquerade principle.

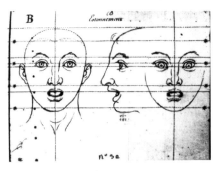

Charles LeBrun, *Astonishment,* **1698**

FACE VALUE

The post-*Thriller* face then, was one which progressively arrived at nearly snow-white skin. The hair remains pitch black and the eyes are dramatically edged in black eyeliner and mascara applied to both the top and bottom lashes. The eyebrows, too, are shaded in as completely black. The mouth receives red lipstick and the chin is fitted with a cleft. There is a curious part in the hair at an angle leaping from the forehead and ringlets of black hair seem pasted on as ersatz sideburns. The eyes tend to dominate the face through their outline and sheer size; Jackson's wide eyes have always revealed white all round the pupil as did those of Diana Ross. Jackson's eyes henceforth become so emblematic that the next album cover for *Dangerous* will only feature his eyes on the cover, peering out from a mask of carnival imagery. Charles LeBrun, in his graphic study of human expression, "saw in the eyebrows real pointers registering the character of the emotion or passion."[11] He set various faces on a Cartesian framework of regulating lines to plot out a range of eyebrow movement and poses.

E.H. Gombrich, in his essay *The Mask and the Face: the Perception of Physiognomic Likeness in Life and in Art,* points out that the simplified portrait has been favoured by artists and photographers since the Mona Lisa.

> Photographers such as Steichen have aimed at a similar advantage by a combination of lighting and printing tricks... and graphic artists, such as Félix Vallotton in his portrait of Mallarmé, have also aimed at similar effects of simplification, much discussed at the turn of the century. We enjoy this game and we rightly admire the painter or the caricaturist who

can, as the saying goes, conjure up a likeness with a few bold strokes, by reducing it to essentials.[12]

Jackson's face, a white ground with black strokes drawn upon it, is such a living example of the graphic Gombrich describes. His face is simplified and pushed towards high contrast to be easily recorded not only on film, but by all visual media. Diagrammatic, with no middle tones, his face is easy to remember and retrace. When asked to sketch a self-portrait, Jackson created a line-drawing of himself as Mickey Mouse. If Jackson's purpose were to become white racially, why then are the eyebrows, eyelashes and hair retained as pure black? These features are constructed for effects entirely distinct from race per se. The face is abstracted, made like a drawing, reproducible and iconic. Its chief benefit is that it can be identified at a distance, all the way from the back row.

When Derrida writes on Mallarmé's *Mimique*, a piece about Pierrot, he focuses on the artificial whiteness of the figure's face. "The blank – the other face of this double session here clarifies its white color-extends between candid virginity ('fragments of candor' ... 'nuptial proofs of the Idea') of the white (candida) page and the white paint of the pale Pierrot who, by simulacrum, writes in the paste of his own make-up, upon the page he is..."[13] The white face's relationship to paper is part of a larger construct of whiteness for Derrida in *White Mythology*. Charles Riley points to the significance of colour in the philosopher's work. "Two signature tones weave their way through Derrida's strangely consistent career: the white of paper and the brilliant gold of van Gogh, coins, and picture frames. White and gold share the qualities of elemental purity and marginality, belonging to the borders of texts and works of art."[14]

F lix V allotton, *Mallarm* , 1895

The mime face with all its attendant significance is not lost on Jackson, an admirer of Marcel Marceau. Recently, Jackson attended the unveiling of a wax likeness of himself – an updated version of Madame Tussaud's – at the Musée Grevin. Making a bizarre triptych, Jackson and Marceau posed for photographs with the wax Jackson standing between them. Here one sees Derrida's 'double session' face alongside the simulacrum. Marceau imitating the minstrel clown, Jackson imitating Marceau, and the waxwork imitating Jackson imitating Marceau. Yet the photograph makes clear the mime face does not entirely account for Jackson's. Other stage traditions might better inform an understanding of his face and its symbolic content.

KABUKI

White greasepaint for the face has been favoured by the stage both in the East and West. Eighteenth-century European theatre is synonymous with white-faced actors in wigs and false beauty marks. The tradition was so strong it leapt from the stage to the audience and became part of male and female beauty regimes. Nowhere has theatrical whiteness held more sway than in the Japan. Kabuki was 'perfected' in the seventeenth century and remains popular today. It is a theatre entirely built around the white face, the *oshiroi*, and a system of choreographed poses, called *kata*.[15] Like Elizabethan theatre, it consisted of an all male cast playing male and female roles. The elaborate Kabuki costumes, wigs and make-up partly serve to make the female characters more believable. However, the best known roles in Kabuki turn out to be those that intentionally focus on the artificiality of gender difference on stage. The female impersonator or *onnagata* is the most celebrated.

> Probably the most outstanding example of stylization in Kabuki, the *onnagata* (also called *oyama*) is a man who typifies the essence of femininity more effectively than would an actress playing the same role. Because of the long tradition behind female impersonation in Kabuki, a set of conventions for representing females has been established which even a female performer would have to follow in playing a Kabuki role.[16]

Whereas a Shakespeare play might include men passing for women or vice versa – made all the more confusing given that the cast was all male – as a secondary or comedic subplot element, many Kabuki plays focus on this aspect. The Kabuki face receives various make-up treatments after the *oshiroi* is applied. *Mebari* are eyeline styles. "Each role-type emphasizes the line of the eyes in a different manner. The eyes are generally made to look larger than normal."[17] Even more Jacksonian are the wig styles which stipulate dressing the black hair with oil to render a high shine with distinctive sidelocks heavily oiled and made stiff. His cleft chin and highlighted cheekbones might be read as *Kumadori* or 'taking the shadows' of the face, a Kabuki tradition borrowed from China.

If Jackson can be said to be trying to pass, it is not as a white, but as a Kabuki actor or an *onnagata*. His recent music video, *Scream*, featuring Jackson along with his sister Janet in a white spaceship, includes several shots of him in a kimono meditating in a virtual rock garden. Other scenes of the video juxtapose Michael's image with Japanese animé.[18] With *Scream*, Jackson's Kabuki face is made fully manifest, all middle tones are drained away, it is a face of just black lines on a white ground. Janet seems to stand in as a foil for her brother, a shadow of his former self. By this time in his career, Jackson has created a set of particular dance movements that, not in their substance but in their standardised serial deployment, reflect the *kata* range of moves and poses. The Kabuki face achieved, there remains yet one more face to appropriate in this whiteness trajectory.

NO

Jackson's latest project is not a music video, but a short film titled *Ghosts*. Essentially a *Thriller* revisited, it allows Jackson to put his new face through various radical changes. In the film, Jackson is a recluse living in a haunted house. When a mob comes to evict him, led by a heavy-set white mayor (also played by Jackson), he conjures a chorus of assorted ghouls – jesters, French fops, Japanese maidens – all the stage types he emulates. After these creatures fail to scare the steadfast mayor, Jackson must resort to horrific manipulation of his own face. Jackson is first seen hiding behind a mask of a skull. He later smashes his own face, revealing his skull, and holds his skin out to the audience Michelangelo-style; death of the Epicoene. Jackson's whole body peels away as he does a dance as a skeleton created by plotting his trademark moves on a computer grid, not unlike LeBrun's, and replacing his body with digital bones.

A world of ghost warriors and maidens, the No theatre of Japan precedes Kabuki by two hundred years and is considered the more refined tradition. The most obvious difference between the two is the use of masks in No. These masks are an integral part of the No costume and are highly prized as art objects in and of themselves.

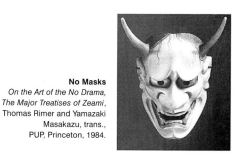

No Masks
On the Art of the No Drama,
The Major Treatises of Zeami,
Thomas Rimer and Yamazaki
Masakazu, trans.,
PUP, Princeton, 1984.

One of the most distinguished features of the Noh theater is the use of masks. As in ancient Greek drama and in the classical Kathakali dance-drama of South India, masks contribute to the stylized quality of the acting and promote and augment the stature and nobility of the characters. [...]

Fifteen varieties of masks for different roles, such as those of the hero, the villain, the demon, the madwoman, specified by the fourteenth- and fifteenth-century masters, still follow traditional usage. They appear again and again on the Noh stage and give the playgoer the complacent pleasure of recognition.[19]

The No mask is predominantly white ground with black or, sometimes, red linework. The demon or ghost masks are more sculptural with high relief brows, hollowed cheeks and protruding cleft chins. Eyeballs are set into the mask, making them appear very large and showing gilt all round the pupils. The whites of Jackson's eyes turn gold in *Ghosts*. The maiden mask is entirely white with black lined eyes and raised brows with a touch of red at the mouth and blackened teeth. Parted black hair is hinted at and is meant to blur the line where the mask abuts the actor's head. The whiteness that is common to all of the No masks reflects beauty standards of the Edo period and before, predating contact with Europeans. Junichiro Tanizaki offers many observations on whiteness in No and Japanese culture: "They cannot have known that a whiter race existed. But one must conclude that something in their sense of color led them naturally to this preference." He explains the tradition of teeth blackening as heightening facial whiteness by contrast. "I know of nothing whiter than the face of a young girl in the wavering shadow of a

69

lantern, her teeth now and then as she smiles shining a lacquered black through lips like elfin fires. It is whiter than the whitest white woman I can imagine."[20]

What makes Jackson's face in *Ghosts* so literally a mask as in No, lies in the lighting of that face and its blatant artificiality. Whereas the *Scream* face is highly stylised, it remains a face under greasepaint, a mask of sorts, more like a Kabuki face. The *Scream* face is intensely lit, but the *Ghosts* face is presented in shadows. Lighting is central to Tanizaki's comparison of Kabuki and No.

> But the Kabuki is ultimately a world of sham, having little to do with beauty in the natural state. The women of the No, portrayed by masked actors, are far from realistic; but the Kabuki actor in the part of a woman inspires not the slightest sense of reality. The failure is a result of excessive lighting.[21]

In the dark environment of the *Ghosts* set, so like the No stage in this sense, Jackson's face appears lighter than his racially white face when playing the mayor. His face is supra-white, the whiteness Tanizaki imagines. Facial transformations in *Thriller* swiftly changed Jackson's face to zombie or wolf-man, while the transformations in *Ghosts* linger on the transformation process itself, the face's seeming elasticity and endless mutability. Of all the manipulations the *Ghosts* face endures – stretching, peeling, shattering – the most arresting effect shows the face crumbling, falling like sand on to the white and black tile floor. Jackson's face, his greasepaint face, erodes like so many layers of old, dry make-up, revealing nothing beyond, not even a skull, as though his head were entirely made out of powder. In other words, his Kabuki face is shown to be false, a mask, a face of No.

After Jackson's face disintegrates, his body rests on the floor for a moment and then collapses in a heap of chalky dust. This vanishing is part of what defines a ghost in Japanese mythology. William LaFleur writes in *Hungry Ghosts and Hungry People: Somaticity and Rationality in Medieval Japan*, "Invisible bodies, no doubt by definition, can be done away with much more easily than visible ones. Since angels, ghosts, demons, ancestors, ghouls and the like take up no physical space in our empirical world, the liquidation of them involves no bloodletting, leaves no corpses, and calls for no official inquiry."[22] Not only is Jackson's face a No mask – some combination of a ghost maiden and a demon – his very body is shown to be ghostlike. So there is no surprise when he appears reanimated in the next scene. He is, after all, a ghost himself, just one of many inhabiting the haunted house.

The *Ghosts* narrative is a reworking of any number of No plays, complete with specters, masks and inky lighting. In this tradition, Jackson's face is apt, if not perfect, for the part. Jackson's face, rather than a disfigurement, is determined by the stage on which he has performed since childhood. His face aims at being racially white as much as the face or mask of the Japanese theatre does. Jackson's face is part of a whiteness project of the theatre of which No is only one extreme iteration. Dyer is right to question assumptions made about Jackson's face as that face is, in the end, an extraordinary mask fashioned in flesh, make-up and digital effects, inoculated against the vicissitudes of lighting and the preferences of film

1 Richard Dyer, *White*, Routledge, London, 1997, p. 50.

2 Donald Bogle, *Toms, Coons, Mulattoes, Mammies, & Bucks, An Interpretive History of Blacks in American Films*, 3rd ed., Roundhouse Publishing Ltd., Oxford, 1994, p. 160.

3 Ibid. p. 127.

4 Jan Nederveen Pieterse, *White on Black, Images of Africa and Blacks in Western Popular Culture*, YUP, New Haven, 1992, p. 135.

5 Ibid. p. 134.

6 Jacques Lacan, "From Love to Libido.", *The Four Fundamental Concepts of Psycho-Analysis.* Jacques-Alain Miller, ed. Alan Sheridan, trans., WW Norton & Co., New York, 1978, p. 193.

7 Camille Paglia, *Sexual Personae, Art & Decadence from Nefertiti to Emily Dickinson,* Penguin, New York, 1992, p. 165.

8 Ibid. pp. 360-361.

9 "HIStory" album (1995) liner notes.

10 "The Columbus Dispatch". Columbus, Ohio. 24 February 1996, p. 2E.

11 E.H. Gombrich, "The Mask and the Face: The Perception of Physiognomic Likeness in Life and in Art.", *The Image & the Eye, Further Studies in the Psychology of Pictorial Representation,* Phaidon, London , 1982, pp. 106-107.

12 Ibid. pp. 118-119.

13 Jacques Derrida, *Dissemination.* Barbara Johnson, trans., UCP, Chicago, 1981, p. 195.

14 Charles A. Riley, *Color Codes, Modern Theories of Color in Philosophy, Painting and Architecture, Literature, Music, and Psychology,* University Press of New England, Hanover, NJ, 1995. p. 163.

15 *The Art of Kabuki, Famous Plays in Performance*, Samuel L. Leiter, trans., UCP, Berkeley, 1979.

16 Ibid. p. 258.

17 Ibid. p. 276.

18 "Scream". Michael Jackson & Janet Jackson. EMI Music Publishing, 1995.

19 Akhtar Qamber, *Yeats and the Noh, with two plays for dancers by Yeats and two Noh plays* [translated by Ezra Pound, 1959], John Weatherhill Inc., New York, 1974, p. 52.

20 Junichiro Tanizaki, *In Praise of Shadows*, Leete's Island Books, Stony Creek, CT, 1977, p. 33.

21 Ibid. p. 27.

22 William R. LaFleur, "Hungry Ghosts and Hungry People: Somaticity and Rationality in Medieval Japan." *Fragments for a History of the Human Body, Part One.* Michel Feher, ed., Zone Books, New York, 1989, p. 271.

Astonishment and *Mallarmé*, from "The Mask and the Face: the Perception of Physiognomic Likeness in Life and Art", in *The Image and the Eye, Further Studies in the Psychology of Pictorial Representation,* E.H. Gombrich, Phaidon, London, 1982, page 107, 119.

No Masks, *On the Art of the No Drama, the Major Treatises of Zeami,* J. Thomas Rimer and Yamazaki Masakazu, Princeton University Press, Princeton, 1984.

73

White and whiteness have a special relationship to orientation, to our position in the world. Mark Wigley, paraphrasing Fernand Léger, states:

> To be faced by white walls is to be lost. [...] While everything is visible in the modern building, vision itself is no longer able to operate. The white surface dislodges the eye in a way that disorients the person that tries to look at it. It reconfigures the very space it is supposed to unify, reconstituting a whole other nightmarish environment.[1]

This disorienting effect of whiteness is often played upon in representations of the lost and the confused. Robert Falcon Scott's journey to the South Pole and the film *Scott of the Antarctic* contain positions of doubt – physical, symbolic, and intellectual – that lend themselves particularly to the strange white environment in which, they actually happened and were filmed.[2] The expedition occurred at the end of the period of classic polar exploration, at a time when the usefulness of such enterprises was being questioned by their main sponsor, the Admiralty. Furthermore, the heroic ideal that appeared to inspire the participants was becoming just that, an ideal, rather than a functioning moral code. Though still strong in the public imagination, it was soon to be drained of serious effect by the bloodletting of World War I. The film, made thirty-five years later in 1948, appeared shortly after another cultural watershed, World War II, and, though in some ways it may be seen as belated war propaganda, I believe it is more of an elegy to an ideal lost in those two wars. The scenes portrayed in the film often betray a backward gaze, a nostalgia for the apparently clear-cut moral imperatives of the pre-war world. At the same time, it suggests that these imperatives, though still to be admired, are no longer completely comprehensible to those who have emerged from these conflicts into the middle of the twentieth century. The film suggests that this ambiguity is not merely the result of history and retrospect gaze, but was present in the original enterprise itself and was part of its tragic failure. The film communicates these discomforting ideas in a number of ways, one of which is the manipulation of landscape and, particularly, the horizon. The 'whiteout', the phenomenon of a snowstorm erasing the horizon in a field of white, is the extreme example of this.

Orientation

orient, v.

**[a. F. orient (11th c. in Littr), ad. L. oriens, orient-em rising sun, east, n.
use of oriens rising , pr. pple. of or_-r_ to rise.]**

1. trans. To place or arrange (anything) so as to face the east...
**b. By extension: To place with the four faces towards the four points of
the compass; to place or adjust in any particular way with respect to
the cardinal points or other defined data; to place or arrange the parts
of a structure in any particular relative position; also, to ascertain the
position of (anything) relatively to the points of the compass, etc.; to
determine the bearings of...**

**2. fig. To adjust, correct, or bring into defined relations, to known facts
or principles; refl. to put oneself in the right position or relation; to
ascertain one s bearings , find out where one is . Also, to assign or
give a specific direction or tendency to...**

**3. intr. To turn to the east, or (by extension) towards any specified
direction. [...]³**

The opening sequence of the film is a series of landscapes, moving picture
and still shots with fairly abrupt transitions. First of sea; then sea and sky;
then of sea, snow, rock and sky; then snow and sky; then of snow only – a
whiteout; then back to snow and sky. In the musical background the strings
swell and the siren chorus disappears, marking the whiteout as the climax of
the series. There is a steady increase in the 'whiteness' of the landscape up to
the climax shot, and also a gradual obliteration of the horizon until it, and
all geographical entities – land, sea, and sky – disappear in a disordered swirl
of snow. These landscapes appear later in the film, and here in the prologue
they foreshadow the polar journey in an ominous way – a way that is yet

filled with light. Light and vision are necessary to orientation and to movement, to journeys on land and narratives on the screen. The first step in
both is the fixing of one's gaze.

IDIOTHETIC ORIENTATION: GAZE AND HORIZON

In the film, when things are going well, the sun shines: when things are
going badly, it clouds over. For most of the hopeful journey towards the
Pole, the weather remains clear and bright. However, once Amundsen's
flag is sighted in the distance, the weather and visibility deteriorate. The
use of 'dirty' weather to communicate distress is common in film. What is
interesting in *Scott of the Antarctic* is that, alongside this convention, a
related phenomenon involving the presence or absence of the horizon
occurs. When goals are clear and decisions obvious, so too is the horizon
– a sharp edge between a clear blue sky and dazzling white snow. When a
character, especially Scott, is perplexed, unsure, in doubt, the snow blows
up and the horizon disappears, or, alternatively, though the weather
remains clear, the camera angle changes so that the background becomes a
horizonless expanse of snow. The net result is the same, a blank white
field without a horizon. This loss of horizon is seen during episodes
characterised by ambiguity or doubt, such as when Scott broadcasts the
scientific goals of the expedition, but telegraphs its importance as a race;
or when the ponies are failing and he is unsure as to when to shoot them;
or when he is in doubt as to which men will go on and which to turn
back; or when he is weighing up the chances of survival on the homeward
journey. In these scenes Scott's sense of confusion and conflict is
signalled by the loss of place on the screen, manifested by the loss of the
horizon. The horizon is an important marker of where-you-are.

The place where-you-are is one's position, and is the starting point for
the process of orientation. It is sensed by the 'orientation triad', which is
comprised of balance, touch, and vision. Balance is the job of the
vestibular apparatus of the inner ear, which senses up, down, and around,
that is, the position of the body in relation to the reference point that is

the earth's gravitational field. Touch, the second component, is of a special type called proprioception. This is supplied by tactile receptors in the muscles of the head and neck. These receptors tell the brain the position of the parts of the body in relation to each other, so that we can maintain our position in relation to external objects despite changes in body, and especially head, position. Vision is the third component and functions at two levels, one below and one above the threshold of awareness. Below the threshold of awareness, vision latches on to certain external objects as points of fixation. The most important of these objects of fixation is the horizon. There is evidence that, at least in some animals, the horizon skyline is recognised and stored, like a snapshot, within the retina itself.[4]

The Vestibulo-Ocular Reflex (VOR) is the name given to the set of physiological mechanisms that co-ordinate the information coming in from the visual, proprioceptive, and vestibular systems. It operates anatomically in the vestibular nuclei, phylogenitically one of the most primitive areas in the brain, and functionally well below the level of awareness. In the most basic terms, it helps us maintain the two necessary components of position, gaze and attitude. Attitude is the position of one's body in space, our position in the world as upright two-legged animals. Conversely, and just as importantly, the VOR allows the world to maintain its position in us. The straightforward way of saying this is that it allows us to maintain our gaze – to keep our eyes fixed on the external object. On fixing the gaze, the VOR takes the information supplied by the vestibular system about where we are in relation to gravity, and feeds this information to the vestibular nuclei to allow the brain to move the head, neck and eye muscles to keep the images of the external world stably fixed on our retinas, despite our own movements or movements of the external objects. It is important to the disorienting effect of whiteness that image stability, gaze, is not due to visual stimuli but to vestibular stimuli.[5] Without the VOR, the world would be the spinning blur we see when stepping off a merry-go-round. The VOR allows us to keep our eye on the prize, whether we are an eagle with a pigeon in our sights, or Scott heading towards a small black flag. It does this without our awareness or any conscious effort on our part.

We can function fairly well, in most circumstances, with the loss of any one of these systems, as in the case of darkness, e.g., finding the toilet in the middle of the night. In darkness, vision is extinguished, and, although this may create some difficulties, the visual sense does not contradict what our other senses are telling the brain, and we can continue to move in a somewhat impoverished, but still navigable, world. On the other hand, when conflicts occur between the inputs from the different systems (as when one steps off a merry-go-round) the effect is very unsettling, very disorienting. Conflicts may also occur because of internal derangements due to disease,[6] or because of the presence of unusual external stimuli, too strong, too weak, or of an unusual type.[7] A whiteout is one of these unusual situations. White does not have the same effect as black.

ALLOCENTRIC ORIENTATION: LANDMARKS AND DEAD RECKONING
This is the level at which the second component of the visual system, operating above the threshold of awareness, enters. Humans are primarily visual creatures; the visual cortex and its connections comprise a large sensory area in the brain. When one wants to 'know' where one is, one consciously looks for a landmark. We always orient ourselves to some visual reference point. The image of that object falling on the retina results in signals being sent to the visual cortex (as well as to the vestibular nuclei). Stimulation of the visual cortex, being functionally above the level of awareness, results in conscious perception of the visual object. This visual object, at the moment it is consciously looked at, also becomes the point of fixation for gaze at the level of the idiothetic system. This combination of point of fixation for gaze and point of reference for orientation makes the object a landmark. A landmark may be any visual object, the main requirement is that it be easily identified. The retina and visual cortex have evolved to identify edges, i.e. the lines along which

areas of greatly differing luminance meet. Here again, we are brought
back to the horizon between earth and sky.

"There is no great secret in arriving in the right spot, it is simply a
matter of travelling in the right direction for the right distance".[8] Dead
reckoning is the navigational procedure we use to move towards a
landmark.[9] It is simply walking from one landmark to another, the route
determined by the capacities of the traveller and the constraints imposed
by the landscape. The landmark is crucial for it becomes, besides the point
of fixation for gaze and the point of reference for orientation, a
navigational beacon, a thing to move towards, a goal, an object of desire.
Dead reckoning sounds easy, and it usually is, but it does require a
landmark.

When there is no object to see, where are we? In the film, when the
last support party turns back, we get an interesting shot of the polar party
disappearing over the horizon. This is done in absolute silence, no
background music, not even any ambient environmental sound. This shot
is particularly effective and affecting. It relies largely on an alternation of
place between presence and absence. This alternation is due to the gradual
disappearance of a landmark from a (suspiciously) poorly defined
horizon. The landmark is the polar party themselves. They are initially 'on'
the horizon, defining it not only in its aspect as the edge between an
almost uniformly white land and a white sky, but also defining it as the
direction of the Pole. As the figures gradually move 'below' the horizon,
they take the horizon with them. We are left staring in the direction of the
Pole at a grey-white blankness of sky and snow, a non-place. Even the
direction is identifiable only because of what has just disappeared from
our view. Without the memory of the now absent polar party, it is not
even a direction. Nothing with which to orient ourselves remains.

INTELLIGIBLE ORIENTATION: MAPS AND POLES

Often we want to be somewhere that we know exists, but that we cannot
see at present. We get there by what a sailor would call 'navigation'.

Navigation is accomplished by employing a series of triads, the first of which is a point of reference, a present position, and a goal. This requires a trio of instruments: a means of measuring direction (compass), a means of measuring distance (sextant), and a map.[10] These tools are then used in the process of triangulation, taking three measurements in the real world of distance and/or direction. If one knows the point of reference or convention the map is based on, one can use it to translate the three measurements taken by triangulation into lines on the map. The point of the intersection of the three lines represents one's present position. This is known as 'fixing a position'. One can then measure on the map the relative direction and distance of the place one wishes to be, plot a course on the map, and, again using the map's convention, translate the course on the map into movement in the real world. The standard format of the navigational map is visual; it is a diagrammatic drawing on a sheet of paper. The map is the link between the visible and the intelligible worlds, and, in a way, it is a continuation of the link vision forges between the worlds of sensation below the threshold of awareness and perception above it.

The major difference between dead reckoning and navigation is that, in navigation, the landmark is shattered into its functional components. In dead reckoning, the visible landmark is the object of fixation for the gaze, the point of reference for orientation, and the goal of movement. In navigation, the object of fixation (what we are seeing now) is merely an intermediary object somewhere between us and our goal; the point of reference (the pole) is a place defined intelligibly rather than visually; and the goal (where we wish to be) is neither the object of immediate gaze nor the point of reference, but the idea of the desired place. It is the convention upon which the map is based that unites these three aspects of the landmark. This convention is the intelligible concept that determines the relationship between the representation and reality, between the map and where we actually are.

Maps involve a number of conventions, the most obvious of which are scale, projection, symbol, and orientation. Although all are necessary, it is orientation that makes a map a thing that is not a drawing. The prime requirement of any map is that one be able to orient it, that is, position it in relation to the real world in a consistent and meaningful way. To do this one must orient it to some thing in the real world, a point of reference that remains the same, time after time, regardless of one's actual position. This point of reference is the pole.

The film *Scott of the Antarctic* is the story of the race for the South Pole, an ambiguous, unknown, strangely imperceptible place, yet one of the twin reference points from which all other places on earth are reckoned and mapped.[11] The poles, in spite of being identifiable, and in spite of being points we use to get us, successfully, from New York to London, are intelligible facts – they are the points at which the earth's imaginary axis of rotation emerges from its real surface. They do not exist as tactile or visual objects. Furthermore, it is in the most lifeless, featureless, coldest, and whitest places on earth, that they do not, in their way, exist. That these places are white is, perhaps, an uncanny coincidence, in that white is also one of those strange things, like the poles themselves, that does not exist in a rather special way.[12]

In the film, a map is used in the scene where Scott is giving the lecture to raise money. This is another episode in which the ambiguity of the expedition's purpose, science versus race, is telegraphed. Though Scott's speech is in support of the scientific goal of the expedition, his behaviour towards the map indicates that it is really a race. A map is also prominent in the Antarctic hut when Scott is outlining the plans for his attack on the Pole to the expedition members. Here the scene is linked to the arrival of the news of Amundsen's expedition, and further insincere reassurances by Scott to Wilson of the scientific goals of their own expedition. (This takes place during a snowstorm and is filmed without horizons.) The maps used in these scenes are gnomic projections of the South Pole, with the landmass coloured in white and the sea in blue. The whiteness of the landscape is the snow that covers its surface, and it becomes an expression of the emptiness of the landscape. This whiteness is transferred onto the map to communicate this blankness, and does seem to signal the specialness and ambiguity of the poles themselves.[13]

WHITEOUT

The whiteout is an unusual natural phenomenon that tests the capacities of all three orientation systems. The blizzard that Oates disappears into, and that keeps Scott, Wilson and Bowers fatally tent-bound is a whiteout. In a whiteout, land and sky appear to disappear: it is like being suspended in a bottle of milk. Actually land and sky do not disappear; land and sky still exist, but they are the same, what has disappeared is the horizon. It is an unpleasant and eerie sensation, caused by the orientation triad of the idiothetic system sending conflicting messages to our brain. Though our vestibular system senses that we are upright, and our proprioceptive system that our head and eyes are in the correct positions, our visual system is deceived. The retina continues to be stimulated, but, at the level of the VOR, there is no horizon, nothing to fix our gaze upon. This is all below our threshold of awareness. We sense that 'something is wrong' and this is manifested by nausea, dizziness and, often, feelings of anxiety, dread, depersonalisation, and an urge to cast oneself forward.[14]

At the allocentric level, the visual cortex continues to be stimulated, but again there is conflict. What we perceive conflicts with the world we are habituated to and know. We see what we know cannot be – a place in which there is something, whiteness, but a place that is no place: it has neither above nor below, front nor back, right nor left.[15] Disorientation thus occurs due to conflicting inputs within each level of the system, and between levels of the system. The disorientation produced by this phenomenon of whiteness has consequences in the real world; people do become lost and and in so doing lose their lives. There is a way out though. In dealing with the altered world of the whiteout, what is required is a restructuring of one's view of reality. One must give up one's usual reliance on the idiothetic and allocentric systems, on sensation and on visual landmarks, and trust entirely to the intelligible. One must ignore the information supplied by one's senses, and rely on map and compass. Though the technical procedures for accomplishing this are not difficult, the leap of faith that needs to be made is. However, it does work. One can reorient oneself and arrive at one's goal.

The polar party dies in a whiteout. This blizzard is the climax of the film. The scenes portraying the death of Oates and the deaths of the other three echo each other. Oates's death, from a dramatic point of view, is much more tightly and effectively managed than the later deaths. The scene begins with a close-up of Oates's blackened face and cracked lips as he awakes. He gets up, and leaves the tent accompanied by the irony of, "I am just going outside and may be some time." There are close-ups of the faces of the others watching him go. It then cuts to the storm outside and Oates limping away from us. The music swells to the same crescendo of strings as in the whiteout of the prologue and Oates disappears through the wall of whirling snow. Whiteout dissolves to black and a voice-over of Scott, "A brave man and a gallant gentleman", then to a shot of the night sky with a very sharply demarcated horizon lit by the *aurora australis*. The deaths of the other three soon follow, but almost as a dénouement.

WHITENESS AND DISORIENTATION

Scott was unable to see the world in any way other than that to which he had become accustomed by his class, education, sex and nationality. He died loyal to his vision of the world, and he died because of it. In a sense, it is this unquestioning loyalty to which this film is both elegy and memorial. In 1948, it was a virtue that no longer pertained. It was lost on the battlefields of the two world wars, but, like the dead, it was still mourned. As we see Scott's tent engulfed by the whiteout, we see the sad, and ultimately pathetic death of not just three men, but of a system of values. Oates' death is different. It is also engendered by loyalty, but not loyalty towards an outmoded system. His loyalty is towards individuals, towards the men in the tent. His continued being puts theirs in jeopardy. Oates, in his last minutes, is not lost. The snow obscures nothing. The horizon he has set his eyes on is not the visual horizon that separates earth and sky, but the ontological one that divides being. The map and convention Oates is using, is of a different order than the one we see Scott pencilling into his notebook as he charts the distances to One Ton Depot. In a way Scott would never be able to do, Oates chose as his landmark, not a geographical feature, but an ethical, perhaps even aesthetic one, death, and he physically performed this decision through an act of navigation. Oates sets off through the howling whiteness towards something, a thing suggested by the aurora-lit horizon that reappears in the last shot of this sequence. Scott will always be mourned because he remains perpetually eleven miles short of his goal: Oates because he reached and crossed it. I am not saying this is what actually happened, but this is what underlies the legend, and the legend which the film memorialises.

The whiteness of these deaths is not serendipitous, either historically or dramatically. It did, in fact, kill these men. In the film, it is consciously used to erase the horizon and confound sense of place so as to signal the ambiguity, confusion and lack of direction that led to their deaths. In a similar manner, white, though it is a symbol of disorientation and absence, is not a simple convention; its effect is based on a physical event and a physiological response. Art exploits this phenomenon of whiteness to communicate disorientation, a thing, perhaps, more effectively felt than thought, seen than said.

1   Mark Wigley, *White Walls, Designer Dresses: The fashioning of modern architecture*, MIT Press, Cambridge, Mass. 1995, p. 231.

2   *Scott of the Antarctic*. Dir. Charles Frend. Prod. Michael Balcon. Ealing Studios, 1948.

3   *The Oxford English Dictionary*, 2nd edn, CD-ROM, Oxford UP, Oxford, 1992.

4   Robert Wehner, B. Michel, and P. Antonsen, "Visual navigation in insects: coupling of egocentric and geocentric information." *J Exp Biol* 199, 1996, pp. 129-140, (p. 129).

5   To demonstrate the VOR in action:

   a. Keep your head still, and shake your hand quickly side to side in front of you. The image of your hand is blurry.

   b. Now keep your hand still and move your head from side to side. Even when the speeds are about the same, the image of your hand is much crisper.

   In the second condition, information from the vestibular apparatus is integrated with visual information to provide much faster responses for the eye muscles.

6   Motion sickness, vertigo, looking down from a very great height, virtual reality simulator sickness, some drug and alcohol effects.

7   Steve McQueen's *Drumroll* and *White Elephant* both use effects induced by vestibular-visual mismatch.

8   Tim Bartlett, *The Royal Yacht Association Book of Navigation*, 1996, Adlard Coles Nautical, London, 1998, p. 155.

9   Dead reckoning from 'deduced reckoning' is the term used commonly to mean navigation using what is perceived with vision, but it does have different technical meanings within different disciplines. For geographers it is how one determines estimated position by calculating distance and direction already travelled; for physiologists it is idiothetic navigation.

10 There are some very interesting things that might be said about the instruments used to measure direction and distance – magnetic compass, log, watch, sextant, odometer, gyrocompass, radar, satellite – the concepts they are based on, and the different ways they are used in ascertaining position, but for the time being perhaps it is best to confine myself to the map.

11 The poles are the points of reference for all modern maps. Initially the point of reference for maps was the rising sun. Thus, maps were *oriented* towards the east.

12 Although visible light is made up of a set of frequencies encompassed by the white spectrum, there is no single frequency of white, as there is for a particular shade of red or blue or green.

13 There is an interesting ambiguity involved in knowing when, and when not to, capitalise the word 'pole'. It is capitalised when referring to the particular location, but remains in small case when referring to the concept. It is often hard to tell which is which, and prior usage is not very helpful.

14 That these feelings have similarities to those experienced in motion sickness, vertigo, looking down from a very great height, etc. should come as no surprise as these states are also situations in which there are conflicting messages being supplied by the orientation triad.

15 When there is confusion between what is felt and what is seen; what is seen and what is known, language invokes the disorienting whiteness of clouds and fog and snow and light. "One's vision is clouded", "lost in a fog", "has one's head in the clouds", "is dazzled", "completely snowed": all involve confusions, misapprehensions, disorientations.

white

(colloq.) innocent, untainted

shit

a contemptible person or thing

OXFORD ENGLISH DICTIONARY

POLLUTION OF THE WHITE CUBE, AKA SHIT HAPPENS
MARY KELLY'S POST-PARTUM DOCUMENT

KATHY BATTISTA

INTRODUCTION[1]

The definitions above represent connotational meanings of the words described. Although white is a word that corresponds to the colour of an object – that is, a physical characteristic – it has been imbued with a powerful ideological function. The same can be said of the expletive shit, which is most frequently used as slang for the word faeces. How did these words come to represent more than tangible qualities when they are both based on physical traits? This paper will examine one case that touches upon the topics of whiteness and pollution, and the ever-changing and problematic definition of those terms.

The example presented here is the exhibition of Mary Kelly's *Post-Partum Document* (*Documentation 1*) at the Institute of Contemporary Arts in London in 1976 [refer to colour plate 1]. An extensive piece of work which took years to create, it consists of series of objects (with accompanying text and charts) that correlate to a child's development from infancy into language. It was a section in which dirty nappies were exhibited with notes regarding the baby's daily intake of food that caused an outrage in the press and mass media, who seized upon the image of soiled garments. Kelly was reviled by tabloid writers and conservative critics who felt that Arts Council funds were supporting an artist and an institution who were jointly arrogant enough to display faeces on the white walls of the gallery.

The most interesting aspect of this episode is its origins. Kelly, an artist whose work has been informed by the women's movement, was by all accounts not deliberately trying to shock viewers who were accustomed to the pristine whiteness of gallery space. Differing from many of her female colleagues at that time, Kelly resisted using her body in the work and her use of abjection was in contrast to feminist artists who attempted to deal with taboo subjects in much more visually disruptive ways. Kelly's incorporation of psychoanalytic theory[2] and the presentation of the work were much more subversive than the nappies seized upon by tabloid press. Fixated by the fact that *Post-Partum Document* incorporated shit into its material composition, they neglected to see the most significant issue: the development of a practice in which the feminist theory was inherent to the art-making process rather than a celebratory[3] reason to make work.

This paper will examine work by various feminist artists that defiled what was generally understood to be the white male space of art

institutions. Many of these pieces were created as part of the revolt
against what some feminists saw as the simple and clear-cut problem of
patriarchy. First I will briefly discuss the ideology behind the white gallery
space. Next I will examine works by American artist Judy Chicago, a
leading figure of the West-coast women's movement in art in the
seventies, and whose aggressive work paved the way for many feminist
artists of following generations. In the final section I will attempt to
contextualise Mary Kelly's less intentional subversion of whiteness
through her aesthetic practice.

THE WHITE CUBE

Galleries today, as most people would think of them and expect them to
be, are primarily white. Many writers have investigated the subject of
whiteness in architectural space[4] and the notion of the white cube[5] is
ubiquitous. This, however, is a post-war Western phenomenon that has
two trajectories at its roots: the evolution of collections of art and the
cultural imperative of the avant-garde. It is common knowledge that the
first collections of art were not shown on white walls, nor were they
aimed at the education of the general public, as they are today.[6]

Brian O'Doherty explains the architect's paring down of the
gallery space in his groundbreaking essay on the white cube: "The ideal
gallery subtracts from the artwork all clues that interfere with the fact that
it is 'art'. The work is isolated from everything that would detract from its
own evaluation of itself."[7] O'Doherty describes the white walls as serving
a functional and neutral role, providing the optimal setting for viewing
works of art. The white walls, however, are not neutral. As Mark Wigley
illustrates, the white coat of paint transforms a space into a sacred or
transcendental area. This white space of the gallery is imbued with the
controlling power of an authority of good taste.

FEMINIST POLLUTION OF THE WHITE CUBE

If the white terrain of the gallery can be said to be a masculine controlled and ordered space, it is essential to look at examples of women who attempted to renegotiate this space. Certain feminist artists attempted to undermine what they read as the patriarchal authority of the white cube, creating alternative exhibition spaces and showing works that did not conform to notions of hygiene and propriety. During the seventies, the reign of Conceptual artists such as Art & Language, Dan Graham, Joseph Kosuth and Lawrence Weiner was beginning to be challenged by feminist[8] artists in Europe and the United States. While their male counterparts relied increasingly upon theoretical notions, feminist artists were creating work in diametric opposition to the cool detachment of Conceptual art. Some feminist artists reacted against this by incorporating their bodies into the work of art.[9] Resisting preconceived notions of the depiction of the female body, feminist artists concentrated on imagery previously deemed inappropriate to the sphere of art, and normally taboo in art history.[10] Works such as Karen LeCocq's *Feather Cunt* (1971), and Faith Wilding's *Womb* (1971) use straightforward vaginal imagery in an assault on the viewer's preconceived notions of good taste and decorum. Both images would be considered pornographic outside of the sphere of art or anatomical study. LeCocq and Wilding cleverly manipulate the transcendental qualities of the white cube to instill the work with a powerful meaning, while subverting the hitherto acceptable notions of female propriety.

An extreme example of this is Judy Chicago's *Dinner Party* (1979), a triangularly shaped installation with thirty-nine place settings representing women who have made important contributions to history such as Virginia Woolf, Georgia O'Keefe and Elizabeth I. Chicago employed stereotypically feminine techniques such as needlepoint and porcelain painting. Each plate relies on vaginal imagery and the installation is a monolithic triangular form, mimicking the shape of the vulva. *The Dinner Party* was re-examined during an exhibition of this and other work by fifty artists inspired by it at the Armand Hammer Centre in Los Angeles. Amelia Jones, curator of the exhibition, writes, *"The Dinner Party* makes clear, the exploration and reclaiming of women's sexuality has most often taken place within feminist art practice through the representation or enactment (through performance) of the female body."[11] Chicago and her colleagues laid important groundwork for later generations of feminism. For them, it was necessary to mount an attack on the preconceived notion of purity in art by reclaiming the female body as valid subject matter. This implicitly included an assault on the masculine-controlled art market, which included the white cube.

Chicago's massive project, premiered at the San Francisco Museum of Modern Art in 1979, was not well received by critics. Hilton Kramer wrote that *"The Dinner Party* reiterates its theme... with an insistence and vulgarity more appropriate... to an advertising campaign than to a work of art" and Kay Larson noted that it "manages to be brutal, baroque, and banal all at once."[12] Critics understood the piece as an affront to the hitherto sacrosanct space of the gallery, with Chicago literally using the female sex organ as a weapon. Although it was not as vituperative as Kramer would have liked to suggest, this breach of pristine whiteness was an essentialist and confrontational result of what feminists understood as the lack of female recognition in history. Chicago's examination of the female condition,[13] and primarily the physical aspects of the female body, unfortunately isolates itself from the larger questions of how to achieve equality between the sexes.

Orifices of the female body, traditionally only shown in religious paintings whose subjects' mouths are represented open in spiritual ecstasy, became subject matter for feminist artists in the seventies. Intimate borders of the body were exploited by artists including Chicago, who for example, presented menstruation as an aesthetic idiom. Art critic Lucy Lippard wrote, "A good deal of this current work by women, from psychological makeup pieces to the more violent images, is not so much masochistic as it is concerned with exorcism, with dispelling taboos, exposing and thereby diffusing the painful aspects of women's history."[14] Chicago's *Red Flag* (1971), depicts a close-up of the artist's torso, truncated from the pubic area to her thighs, while removing a bloody tampon.[15] In its aggressive attack on notions of feminine propriety, it also attacks notions of aesthetic purity.

Chicago's *Menstruation Bathroom* was exhibited in 1972 at Womanhouse, an artist-run initiative in which a house was remodelled and used as studio and exhibition space, in California.[16] What appears to be an immaculately scrubbed bathroom has been contaminated by used sanitary napkins and tampons with additional feminine products featured on the shelves. Chicago's blatant display of female detritus provokes viewers in a direct transgression of the white cube ideology. *Menstruation Bathroom* was exhibited in a domestic space transformed into a gallery. Understanding that it was unlikely that another gallery would show such a work at that time, Chicago and her collaborators created their own exhibition space, which mocked the traditional notions of a white cube.

Chicago is one of many American feminist artists, who admittedly had reason to react against a male dominated arts establishment, and used confrontational and provocative imagery in defiance of patriarchal terms. A large body of the work made involved transgressing modes of decorum and previously taboo issues, specifically within the space of a gallery, be it traditional or alternative. There was the danger, however, of marginalising themselves by using terms that only the feminine sex could relate to. Was there an alternative to defiling (physically and metaphysically) the white, pure space of a gallery, and using body-oriented imagery, the same thing that many of the artists were reacting against in the work of a predominantly male art history? Perhaps an examination of the development of an art practice that was informed by feminism as seen in the work of Mary Kelly can provide answers to this question.

When Mary Kelly's *Post-Partum Document* was shown at the ICA in 1976 it caused outrage in the national press. The headline of the *Evening Standard* boldly stated, "On show at ICA... dirty nappies!" The article continued to elaborate, "Taxi drivers and other forthright citizens may have a blunt answer for it. But the question 'Are dirty nappies art' is now demanding a serious answer."[17] Despite the class ridden humour of the sentence the tabloid writer gets to the heart of a question that has been plaguing art since the beginning of the European avant-garde: what is the autonomy of a work of art? Since Duchamp surreptitiously displayed a urinal in the gallery space, the question of what constitutes a work of art and a debate around authorship have been a nagging problem for critical discourse as well as society in general. Mary Kelly's work, although unreputedly of her authorship, elicits similar reactions. Critics and the art establishment would not have questioned whether this was a work of art, but they did dismiss it as a piece "just about a woman and her baby."[18] The hostile reception of the piece in the popular press highlights the crux of the scandal: what makes a child's faeces, an utterly normal by-product of the rearing procedure, inappropriate for gallery walls?

A formalist answer, which would attest to the fact that the brown in the dirty nappies was in contrast to the clean white walls, falls short when one is reminded that aesthetically the nappies have similar qualities to those of abstract paintings. Another argument could be the hygienic reasons for the inappropriateness of dirty nappies. This, too, is unfounded as the nappies were in frames, exhibited as professionally and as slickly as Kelly's more commercially minded colleagues. What then is it about the object that is so offensive? Any informed hypothesis would require an in-depth analysis of the status of taboo objects in Western culture. Influenced by the avant-garde and Modernist theory, purity and hygiene remain holy in Western culture. The nappies, however, were not meant as an affront to the high esteem of the white cube, but were a side effect of a carefully devised and articulated body of work.

Kelly's ambitious and seminal work, like Chicago's *The Dinner Party*, was also re-examined after two decades in an exhibition where it was represented.[19] What strikes most in the reclamation of these works is the difference between Kelly's research and that of her American colleagues. Kelly's immersion in the women's liberation movement in London, and in particular the History Group,[20] a collective that took a theoretical approach to the issue of women's inequality, had a profound effect on her work. The members the group concentrated on the dissemination of feminist discourse. This included an investigation of the Freudian and Lacanian psychoanalysis that would surface most significantly in Kelly's *Post-Partum Document*.

Mary Kelly did have a feminist agenda as did the other artists discussed above. However, it did not seem that her specific intention was to make a work of art that would politicise and de-masculinise a gallery space. *Post-Partum Document* is the result of an intricate and detailed examination of the mother's role informed by psychoanalysis, especially the work of Freud and Lacan. Kelly's involvement in various reading groups, including the History Group, introduced the use of psychoanalysis to the artist. Lacan's writings about the female's inherent lack of a phallus, and subsequent desire to attain one through the birth of a child, informed the work as well as her interest in infantile sexuality. An excerpt from a conversation between the artist and Laura Mulvey relates this:

> LM: So that was a little chain, a linked chain beginning with feminism and the way you wanted to shift the center of art, the avant-garde theory of art, out of art itself into what you call 'social purpose'. That brought up questions of the artist, and then with that you come back to the question of sexual identity – the artist as male or female – and this brings you back once again to feminism and to the shift that takes place between your film and *Post-Partum Document*.

MK: *Post-Partum Document*, I think brought those issues into clearer focus for me as an artist. ...What is maternal femininity? How is it constructed in the context of the mother-child relationship?[21]

The conversation illustrates that Kelly, unlike other female artists working in the seventies, was not attempting to shock or disgust. Instead, *Post-Partum Document* is an investigation of the mother-child relationship in its earliest stages as well as the child's entry into language.

The dirty nappies make up a section entitled Documentation I: *Analyzed faecal stains and feeding charts*. They in fact embody only one element of a six-part series that took Kelly five years to complete. The nappies illustrate Lacan's theory of the mother's desire for a healthy baby, the first stage in the mother-child relationship. Used as proof of the health of the child, the nappies are visual evidence of the baby's well-being. Kelly writes in her footnotes to the *Post-Partum Document*: "The normal faeces is not only an index of the infant's health but also within the patriarchy it is appropriated as proof of the female's natural capacity for maternity and childcare."[22] The sexual division of labour, then is examined in Kelly's work, which illustrates the dependence as the mother as primary provider for the child.

Although critics reacted quite strongly to the dirty nappies, this was not the most challenging aspect of *Post-Partum Document*. The true subversion lies in Kelly's appropriation of male theory for a feminist strategy, something that elicited criticism from many of her British feminist colleagues. Using Lacanian theory she manages to undermine the presupposed status of the mother as the primary care provider for a child. This was a clear departure from other female artists, who rejected the male authority altogether. Kelly used the male voice to substantiate a feminist practice, and in doing so coincidentally touched upon the issue of taboo subject matter. While traditional depictions of motherhood by male artists have concentrated on the mother as the main source of imagery, Kelly transfers the iconography to her son, who becomes one of the subjects of the work. The real investigation, however, is the mother's Lacanian desires, which are scrutinised through a male object, her son.

Thus, if Kelly's work was seen as radical by members of the press in 1976, they concentrated on the least interesting aspect of the work – the aesthetic language which included dirty nappies. These dirty nappies, which so enraged journalists, stand in contrast to celebratory feminist work such as Chicago's and LeCocq's that comprised of much more visceral images. While these artists deliberately attempted to pollute the gallery space, and thereby undermine the patriarchy of the white cube, Kelly cleverly managed to develop a practice informed by feminism, which came about as a manifestation of the theory studied in Britain during the seventies.

The nappies incident should not be read as an intentional affront to the male-dominated gallery system. Did it, however, manage to undermine the power invested in the white cube? The predilection for white cube galleries has remained intact. White walls are still *de rigeuar* in gallery spaces throughout the world. Ironically, many of the works by feminist artists that were seen as shocking two decades earlier are now being reclaimed by curators who programme these spaces. Kelly, and her colleagues such as Chicago, made an important contribution to the development of a feminist art practice. Their work paved the way for future generations of women artists to deal with issues of gender, sexuality and space. Contemporary artists such as Sarah Lucas, Elke Krystufek, Shirin Neshat and Tracey Emin[23] are today still struggling with the issues that Kelly and Chicago confronted two decades earlier. The only difference today is that the white cube galleries are more than willing to contemplate controversial work, especially those commercially inclined who reap the profits.

NOTES

1 Please note that this article dates from 1997. Since then there have been numerous, significant contributions to this debate, such as: Laura Cottingham, *Seeing through the Seventies: Essays on Feminism and Art*, G & B Arts International, 2000, Sabine Breitweiser, (ed.); *Rereading PPD Mary Kelly*, E. A. Generali Foundation, Vienna, 1999; Juli Carson "(Re)Viving) Post-Partum Document", *Documents*, Spring 1999.

2 Kelly's work is absolutely dependent upon Freud and Lacan, especially the latter's theories on the child's entry into language. Kelly came to psychoanalysis through the History Group, which will be discussed at further length later in this paper.

3 I must thank Mark Cousins for a useful discussion on this issue. I use the term celebratory to indicate artists whose work centres around the notion of inequality as an essentialist issue solely dependent on gender difference. Essentialist feminists reduced the problem of women's inequality as an example of the omnipotence of patriarchy. Other strands of feminism, in particular socialist and psychoana-lytic readings, recognised partriarchy as a more complex ideology, rooted in the structures of society and in particular the issues of class division, politics and economy.

4 See Le Corbusier, *Towards a New Architecture* , The Architectural Press, London, 1927 and Mark Wigley, *White Walls, Designer Dresses: The Fashioning of Modern Architecture*, The MIT Press, Cambridge, Massachusetts, 1996.

5 See Brain O'Doherty, *Inside the White Cube: The Ideology of the Gallery Space*, The Lapis Press, Santa Monica, 1986.

6 Instead they were private collections that served to emphasize the social status or prestige of the owner. These collections were not open to the public. Entrance was gained only by association with the wealthy patron, which excluded those of lower classes and unattended females. The Louvre Museum, begun in the 1790s, was the first collection to be hung by art-historical arrangement, for the purpose of showing visitors the progress of art and the degrees of perfection to which it was brought

by all those peoples who have successively cultivated it. In the nineteenth and twentieth centuries collections organised and supported by one wealthy magnate became the fashion. (Peggy Guggenheim and Isabella Stewart Gardner are important exceptions, however.) Although these men claimed their collections were in the interest of the public, they were often self-promoting endeavours that benefited their international reputations. For a clear account of this history see Carol Duncan, *Civilizing Rituals: Inside Public Art Museums*, Routledge, London, 1995.

7 O' Doherty, p. 14.

8 I use the word feminist as an umbrella term. As there is not enough space here to deconstruct the various intricately linked, and at times diametrically opposed strands of the movement, I will for now refer to it under the general term feminist.

9 For an excellent examination to body-oriented practice see Amelia Jones, *Body Art: Performing the Subject*, University of Minnesota Press, Minneapolis, 1998.

10 Of course in the history of art

there are examples of 'indecent' imagery, which were created for patrons to enjoy in the privacy of their home. One example is Courbet's *L'Origine du monde (The Origin of the World)*, a truncated depiction of a reclined woman's openly exposed vagina and pubic area, which was executed for a private collector (a Turkish ambassador and collector of erotica) who kept it under a green veil.

11 Amelia Jones, "Sexual Politics: Feminist Strategies, Feminist Conflicts, Feminist Histories in Sexual Politics: Judy Chicago's The Dinner Party" in *Feminist Art History*, UCLA at the Armand Hammer Museum of Art and Cultural Centre in association with the University of California Press, 1996, p. 23.

12 Jones, p. 84.

13 Chicago writes in her autobiography that she was concerned with the question of "What is it to be a woman?" Judy Chicago, *Through the Flower: My Struggle as a Woman Artist*, Penguin Books, New York, 1975, pp. 156-158.

14 Lucy Lippard, "The Pains and

Pleasures of Rebirth" in *The Pink Glass Swan: Selected Feminist Essays on Art*, The New Press, New York, 1995, p. 111.

15 Ironically, in Chicago's *Red Flag* the tampon resembles a phallus, which serendipitously parallels Kelly's interest in psychoanalytic theory, in particular the notion of penis envy.

16 Womanhouse was part of the Feminist Art Program at CalArts that Chicago established with Miriam Schapiro while teaching there in the early seventies. This would be an important springboard for many feminist artists of the next generation.

17 *Evening Standard* 14 October 1976.

18 Lucy Lippard writes of the denigration of *Post-Partum Document* in the mainstream artworld in the forword to Mary Kelly, *Post-Partum Document*, Routledge & Kegan Paul, London, 1983, p. xi.

19 The exhibition of *Post-Partum Document* was accompanied by and archival section entitled "Excavating *Post-Partum Document*: Mary Kelly's Archive 1968-1998" and took place at the EA Generali Foundation in Vienna, September 25-December 20 1998.

20 Founded in 1970 as a consciousness-raising collective, participants included Sally Alexander, Anna Davin, Liz Danziger, Rosalind Delmar, Margarita Jimenez, Mary Kelly, Laura Mulvey, Branka Magas, Juliet Mitchell and Margaret Walters. Kelly's involvement with this group led to her first critical writings, such as a review of the Miss World Demonstration and reviews of films made by Mulvey and her partner Peter Wollen. Obviously she had ties with other groups, such as the Artist Union.

21 "Mary Kelly and Laura Mulvey in Conversation" in Mary Kelly, ed., *Imaging Desire*, The MIT Press, Cambridge, Massachusetts, 1996, pp. 35-6.

22 Kelly, *Post-Partum Document*, p. 41.

23 Emin's *My Bed* exhibited in the 1999 Turner Prize Exhibition at the Tate Gallery, which included blood-stained knickers and used condoms, elicited many references to Kelly's work in the press.

IMAGE CREDIT

Mary Kelly, *Post-Partum Document, Documentation 1*, 1973. Courtesy of artist.

It is a strange prejudice which sets a higher value on depth than on breadth... Yet it seems to me that a feeling such as love is better measured, if it can be measured at all, by the extent of its surface than by its degree of depth.

— Michel Tournier, *Friday*

Refer to colour plate 3.

BEAUTY OF SURFACES/MEMORIES OF WAR

LORENS HOLM

This art was born in a flash of white light. The Tate was damaged on the nights of 15 and 22 September 1940 by bombs targeting the adjacent military buildings (additional hits occurred in January, March, and May of 1941). In the current idiom of war, in which only civilians get killed and not soldiers, the Tate was collateral damage. Recently the shrapnel damage on the outside was listed, so these scars shall be preserved in perpetuity. Imagine that the Trustees were so taken by what they had done that they commissioned a suite of photographs of the shrapnel damage to celebrate the event (the listing, not the bombing), and used them as the centrepiece of an exhibition that also included archival material about the bombing (to give it an aura of respectability). Imagine also that the photographer was so taken by the beauty of the wall that he made all the photographs life size so that he could capture exactly, without diminution or exaggeration, the extraordinary beauty of the marks [refer to colour plate 2]. In his reveries, he imagined that some of them would be displayed opposite the wall, forming a kind of memorial garden or piazza. (It might be paved in limestone just like the wall).

Imagine also that someone was asked to write about this wall. The argument was written only in the presence of photographs, and will only

1. Maimed bodies, Details of stumps and clear eyes, Roehampton Military Hospital, 1918

2 'The seismographic nature of the markings suggested a hand responsive to the most minute variations within the psyche.'
Andre Masson, *Automatic Drawing*, 1924

ever be received in their presence, and not before the wall itself. The photographs, imaginary or not, necessary or not, will always mediate and to some extent interrupt any argument about the beauty of the wall. They are present, even when we do not think we are talking about them. The complicity of the photograph with architecture is the theme of this paper:

The first thing one notices about the shrapnel scars, once one is paused and poised to look at them (the wall?; the photographs?), is that they are incredibly beautiful. We are asked to aestheticise a fragment of the Blitz. The scars have transformed the flank wall of what had been a flaccid beaux-arts pile (with Corinthian pretensions) into a sensuous surface with a dignity and silence approaching the monumental. The shrapnel produced dinnerplate fractures in the limestone around the point of impact, making breast-like craters. The masonry joints function as a grid against which these freer forms float, suggesting the *plan libre* (a Modernist paradigm which has become universal in post-war reconstruction) and implying the co-ordinate system by which these scars might be mapped, transferred, categorised, tabulated, and archived. The scars are a mix of earthy reds, blacks, warm greys, and piss-yellow. The colours overlap like wash. Up close they have the elusive quality of intergalactic dust storms. They have layered the limestone with the streaks and stains of diverted rainwater.

The photographs belong to that familiar genre of war photographs –
perhaps more accurately *aftermath-of-war* photographs – which include
portraits of handsome amputees and *vedute* of quaint towns which look
like piles of bricks. They seem to have become popular after World War
I.[1] Imagine the photographs are arrestingly beautiful. The most striking
fact about them, however, is that they are redundant. This is nowhere
more obvious than in the piazza, where a few of the photographs are
poised directly facing the damage of which they are the portraits. The fact
that these scars have just been listed means that the photographs will
never need to be called upon as record or witness of a past and
irrecoverable event. For unlike Schinkel's Neue Altes Museum, whose
shrapnel scars were cut out and patched with new stone in an attempt to
return it to its historical condition (an assertion of historical-value over
age-value, about which more later), the Tate's scars will be preserved in
perpetuity. Why do we need this paper replacement, when the stone
surface refuses to be replaced? What happens when we are asked to
aestheticise war damage? When we are asked to contemplate the scene of
the crime as if it were a thing of beauty? What relationship do the
photographs have to their objects, and how does their nagging
redundancy return to haunt the wall itself?

A building is a body. It endures in a slumbering lumbering sort of way,
and its surface accrues the traces of events. Buildings are bombed, cut,
gouged, sliced, altered, filled in, added to, subtracted from, painted,
partially cleaned, burnished, have bits screwed onto them, and bits
removed leaving holes, shadows cast onto them, and graffitied. *Graffiti is
beautiful*. They rust, crack, have plants grow in the cracks, have cracks
repaired. Buildings endure, and things are done to them. Buildings are
victims of war, victims of life. Le Corbusier finally threw up his hands
and said "Life is always right," when he could no longer resist the mini-
castle-and-cottage redecorations of his beloved Pessac.[2] The shrapnel
damage falls into the category of things done to the surfaces of buildings.
We are reminded of such epiphanic examples as the Berlin wall in the

agony of its destruction; or why Rome is so much *denser* than Manhattan. It is a question first of how these scars might be understood, and then of how they might be valued.

The phenomenon in the field of modern art which most closely resembles the shrapnel scar, is automatic drawing and all other species of automatism, augury and divination, in which inscriptions from nowhere offer themselves to the wondrous eyes of the artist for interpretation and aesthetic contemplation. Automatic drawing was popularised by the Surrealists, like André Masson who employed a technique of drawing rapidly with no subject matter or composition in mind.[3] Lines react to prior lines. The pen never leaves the paper. By a process of action and reaction, fragments of objects, and hybrids of objects would begin to emerge in the work, as a secondary effect of the materials, surfaces, and gestures. To the extent that Masson relinquished direct and masterly control in these works, the lines begin to engage each other in syntactical relations, and relate more to each other as a horizontal dispersion across a surface than to the hidden objects of authorial intention and reference.

Masson's work was implicated in a cycle of war and war damage, for he developed automatic drawing as a way of exorcising his war demons.[4] He was a damaged warrior, and in many ways, it was the beauty of war that damaged him. In a passage as disconnected as the opening scenes in *Apocalypse Now*:

> There were moments of true happiness even on the line of fire. That is astonishing perhaps… The odour of the battlefield was intoxicating. 'The air was filled with a terrible alcohol.' Yes, Apollinaire saw all of that. There was only one poet to say it… The shock of the dead in strange positions, like those I saw one day seated on a bank of earth, their heads having been blown away by an Austrian 85… Others in very beautiful poses, like the one who had the appearance of a wounded lioness. At first I thought he was still alive and crying out for help.[5]

The Tate was also maimed by war, but it was already maimed. It is only the stump of Sidney R. J. Smith's much more grandiose design, its dome

Refer to colour plate 4.

truncated, its embellishments stripped by an overruling Board of
Trustees.[6] (Even the original design was a disfiguration of the Corinthian
Order.)[7] The Tate damage is a particular instance of a general condition
of the modern city as damaged goods. According to Jean Nouvel, who is
a reader of Deleuze and Guattari and whose work is attentive to surface
characteristics, scarifying, tattooing, and other kinds of writing,
architecture is salvaged from forces beyond its control and, like Masson's
drawing, bears all the traces of this beautiful birth.

> Since the invention of the city as an architectural concept in the 15th
> century, history has constantly shown that the city owes less and less to
> design; but rather that it evolves as the result of the economic forces on
> certain areas, of forces which nothing – let alone aesthetic or humanist
> principles – can withstand… We must face the fact that modern cities
> have invented themselves without us – and sometimes even despite us…[8]

There is a myth that architecture speaks to something contained and
whole and pure which is called a design. But if the modern city and the
conditions which effect the procurement of buildings are no longer
masterable, and if the architect is no longer a master of law, finance,
form, aesthetics, advertising, but operates in an arena too vast, powerful,
and complex to exercise control, then all buildings are victims, and each
one is the result of a design which is damaged, with limbs cut off. All
design is renovation, a modification of the existing. There are no
greenfield sites. Buildings are war orphans, "orphaned because they are no
longer linked to the classical architectural culture which produced
them…"[9]

There is already a nascent architecture of surface inscription and
wounding, which glides upon the work of Deleuze and Guattari. In *The
Logic of Sense*, Deleuze – following Lewis Carroll's fascination with the
Stoics – articulates sense in terms of surface and event. He distinguishes
bodies, substances, states of affairs (nouns, adjectives) which exist in the
present, from effects and incorporeal events (verbs) which do not exist in
the present, but subsist in past and future.[10] Events, or the effects of one

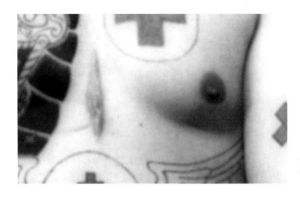

3. Writing on the body
Photo: Randall, *Franko B*

body upon another (his example: the scalpel which cuts flesh, scarification) do not change the nature or substance of bodies. The cut exists only on the surface of the body.

Meaning is a surface event, and contra Plato, idea is an effect on the surface of bodies, not a cause from within. 'Linguistic effects' are superficial. This explains how we might understand Masson's lines as existing in syntactical relations to each other. It also explains how the *things done to buildings* can be incorporated into an architecture, for "events (read *meaning of a building*) are no longer sought in the depths, but at the surface" of things.[11] The inscribed surface is a 'mirror' of events. It also suggests how close the photograph may be to architecture (or to anything), for a photograph is a surface which, like the mirror, only ever records the effects of surface. This architecture of surface inscription will, like the work of Nouvel, have a slightly different relationship to ornament, for ornament is no longer an add-on, but is something inscribed or imprinted in the surface. It disrupts the classical opposition between the essential/structural and the non-essential/decorative,[12] for architecture is mute and identityless before it is marked. Henceforth the shrapnel marks will be referred to as inscriptions.

If this wall is, like Masson's drawings, inscribed by war, and if surface inscription is the way that architecture carries meaning, then how do we account for its beauty without recourse to the psychoanalytic register? For one thing, the Surrealists explicitly tried to link automatic writing to the unconscious, despite a good deal of reticence on Freud's part. Furthermore Melanie Klein, to whom we will return, locates art and architecture within a cycle of love and hate which is relevant to war art and war inscription.

We do not resist these interpretations, but insist that aestheticisation lifts the wall out of these contexts, and places it in the context of art. It is precisely when it is seen as a work of art, that it is no longer just evidence of war, or a hook upon which to fix a memory of war. When it is seen as beautiful – or possibly beautiful – it no longer elicits the response "krauts" or "I forgive you your sins". It is taken out of the context of war, or love, hate, forgiveness, atonement, forgetting, compensation, pay-offs, twentieth-century history, Tate history, German-English relations, neo-Nazis, even art history, or any other narrative, and placed in relation to other works of art, as art. Kant refers to aesthetic judgement as non-appetitive. The "this is beautiful" of aesthetic judgement relates at some level to what pleases, but it does not relate to all the appetites and particular wants and desires which identify each individual and catalogue their history. The "this would look good over my sofa", or "this makes me feel good", or all the other possible reactions we might have to a work of art which individuate our lives and which do not particularly distinguish it from things which are not art, like a new boat or neck tie, about which we could make the same statements.

Refer to colour plate 5.

In so far as this war-inscribed wall is a memorial (and not art), it is both reminder or memory of a war and threat or promise of possible future wars which are out of site/sight (think of the museums of Belgrade). The bomb blast inscribes a surface which records a past and professes a future. Deleuze says that each event looks to the past and future, but is never present in bodies. It splits the present infinitely. (I paraphrase: Alice is getting bigger and smaller at the same time; having just been cut a little and about to be cut more). To the extent that the wall is taken out of the context of art, it is possible for the wall to mobilise the unconscious in a way similar to how the Surrealists understood automatic process to mobilise the unconscious. Automatic drawing, automatic writing, *objêts trouvés*, the wanderings of the *flaneur*, and games of chance were seen to provoke a chain of free associations led by unconscious desire, the same path of displacements which, broadly, Freud travelled to arrive at the unconscious.

Surfaces which we call art exist on multiple levels. Some people will always return to the wall and piazza as a memorial. The people who still bear grudges against the Germans for what they did (most of my father's generation) will always be able to return to the piazza and have a good hate session, or depending upon mood, a cathartic moment where they find relief from the burden of their hate. The wall will always function that way as long as it is still recognised for what it is. Other people may find the breast shaped inscriptions erotic. The recognition that the wall is beautiful – whether by imagining its photographs or other means – will not diminish this capacity. It is just that this capacity is not the aspect of it that is art. When it functions this way, or to the people for whom it functions this way, it may or may not also be functioning as art. When the Pope sticks Postit™ reminders on the walls of the *Stanze*, his Raphaels do not cease to be art and become a notice board, they are both. Architecture has always had to accept this multivalence, this depth. A building may or may not be architecture, but when it is architecture, it is architecture + building, not architecture in place of building. It may provide *commodity* and *firmness* at the same time as *delight. But suddenly you touch my heart and I say "This is beautiful." That is architecture. Art enters in.*[13]

In "Love, Guilt and Reparation", Melanie Klein implicates art in a cycle of aggression, guilt, and reparation which begins with the fantasy of tearing the breast that feeds you, and which structures the relations we enter into with the people we love. Architecture, like any act of love, is a sublimated form of guilt-born reparation. This may be one of the functions of an art object or a building, but it is not the way they function when they are functioning as art. Klein's account recommends itself because it seems to bear a formal relationship to a Deleuzean account of surface meaning. The psychic tropes which animate the cycle of love, hate, guilt and reparation, traverse one smooth surface, because they are not organised hierarchically, but temporally. However, the superficial aspect of Klein's account is disingenuous because guilt and reparation are demonstrably *not* what art is about, not even an aestheticised war inscription, and any attempt to convincingly argue that it is will have to make an accusatory gesture which penetrates beneath the surface, which is reached via interpretation.

It is the nature of art to be always in a tug of war between being art and being something else which is not art: a beautiful inscribed surface versus a building damaged by bombs. This aesthetic tension relates to many other phenomena, which can be mobilised in support of this thesis. These include the tension between surface and depth in Surrealist automatic drawing: on the one hand, we are asked to understand the drawings as syntax, on the other as oracle of the unconscious. It describes the high maintenance, tremulous, rarefied world which Deleuze inhabits, in which meaning as surface is in continuous exchange with more conventional models of meaning. This world seems to be reached only at certain terrifying moments, like aesthetic moments, when a surface becomes art.

This tension also relates to Freudian analysis, in which meaning is at every moment reconstituted on a surface which both reveals an underneath (the unconscious, the latent) through interpretation, and conceals it (without which surface, it would not be unconscious). Freudian analysis acknowledges the complexity of surface and interpretation in a way that Klein's account of art cannot. Thus, at the moment of waking, the dream work constructs an elaborate image which functions like a façade, which is the exterior surface of the dream known to consciousness. Similarly, the screen memory is constructed by the psychic processes as a screen which both conceals and identifies retrospectively constructed originary experiences. Both dream façade and screen memory mark thresholds between the conscious and unconscious processes. Although Freudian analysis appeals to an underneath which explains the surface, each explanation leads to another surface. There is no arrival at a

4. Writing on the body: the
use of livers to map the
universe and to lay out a
town
Etruscan bronze

deep origin, for originary experience is a construct of screen memory and there is no further underneath which is meaningful to the subject. If there is an underneath, it is brute organism, not so different from the underneath of the surface of the war-inscribed wall (mute solid stone). The inside of the wall, behind the inscriptions, is a gallery. It is not the inside of the war inscriptions, in the sense of some kind of privileged access to the meaning of the inscriptions, but only more images. The photographs of the inscriptions, life size, are arranged as closely as possible to positions which correspond to the inscriptions on the outside. The archival material may seem to interpret the photographs in the sense of providing facts associated with them, but in the end, these are just images as well.

MEMORIES OF WAR

Listing acknowledges the historical value of these inscriptions. They are preserved in stone, so that they do not have to be preserved in memory. There is an uncanny sameness between listing and photography: it captures and preserves a moment in history the way the photograph does, and offers it to the viewing public as if it were forever new.[14] Because the photographs are full size, they are as very near to being equivalent to their objects, the shrapnel scars, as they ever will be; except that no bird will ever try to nest in one. They will always be the lesser term in the equation: the same but not the real thing. This redundancy, which is underscored by the fact that listed wall and photograph are seen together, points to a deeper redundancy. They are tiresome doubles.

Both wall and photograph began in a flash of light. The identity could hardly be more literal. The limestone cladding and the photographic paper are both sensitive surfaces; it seems that nothing is gained by replacing the trace of a blast upon the former, with the trace of a flash upon the latter. They are both indexical. The indexicality of the photograph is held up as the most persuasive argument for its value; but it is precisely its indexicality which is the most serious threat to its individuality and uniqueness, and hence to its status as art. A crime scene photograph is valued only because it records an event; it could be replaced by any other photograph which records that event. The shrapnel is the imprint – direct, causal, predating, although not independent of the language which structures signs – of a bomb blast upon a sensitive surface.

The wall already functions the way the photograph functions, and could easily replace it, as a record of the bomb blast. There are urban myths which identify wall and photograph, like the people 'photographed' to the walls of buildings by the bomb flash of Hiroshima.[15] The wall literally behaves as if it were a negative. The shrapnel marks have reversed value over the years, pulling a universe of colours into their depths. The archival photographs show white limestone where the soot-stained surface was chipped away.

Yet the photographs are compelling. Assume the photographs are astoundingly beautiful. The earth tones, the warm greys and whites, float like clouds across the huge glossy saturated surfaces, as if they were some alien landscape with its alien atmosphere, lunar or Martian. They drift free of the conventional anchors of scale, orientation, and composition. The camera plate might be horizontal (topographic) or vertical (perspectival). The surfaces could be huge (craters) or microscopic (pockmarks). Any side could be up. They could be concave or convex, negative or positive. If the photographs were not so compelling, we would not remain so confounded by their redundancy.

The flash of light sectioned the darkness, and produced an image upon a sensitive surface. The bomb left its indelible imprint on the stone. It

5. Architecture erased by its own photogaph
Pierre Vivant, *Tobacco Factory*, Newcastle

marked an instant, its short duration, a fraction of a second, underscoring the fact that that instant will only ever have been either future or past. "Only the present exists in time... But only the past and future inhere in time and divide each present infinitely."[16] That event is now absorbed as surface. Barthes defines a similar dialectic of event and surface with the idea of the 'punctum', the unbearable moment in every photograph which captures an instant of past time, the particular and elusive present of the photograph, as opposed to all the other ideas and messages which might endure upon its surface.[17] The photograph is a time machine which articulates *Becoming-unlimited* (event, meaning, past/future) from *extra-Being*[18] (substance, body, state of affairs, the present). The punctum is analogous to the flash of light that accompanies the shutter-speed. It is a detail, and it is different for every photograph, it might even be different for different viewers of the same photograph. The particular poise of the hands in the lap, the particular angle of the eyes – just here and not there. With the shrapnel damage, we are in the presence of such a punctum. It is exactly this dinnerplate fracture, so deep, precisely here, and not there. If we knew how to read them, if we were forensic specialists, we might be able to define trajectories and determine the position and force of the bomb.

With wall and photograph, we are in the presence of narrative. It is a narrative which began with an unknown pilot in an unknown airfield in Germany, perhaps with a tense meal or in the briefing room, before another night raid over London. That pilot is connected to a family and to the rest of an aircrew, and they to their families. The wall, like the photograph is action arrested, and that action arrested is a section cut through the four-dimensional body of a narrative which proliferates wildly. It marks the intersection of several *genera* of narratives, for there is also the story recorded in the archival material of how Rothenstein, who was living in the basement of the Tate, was awakened from his slumbers. Photographs suggest narratives even when we don't know what they are or cannot reconstruct them.

At the same time, the photographs serve the purpose of lifting the marks out of the context of these narratives of war and re-presenting them as pure surface. This fluctuation in and out of narrative is another way of stating that which we have maintained to be the precondition of art: the object considered as art always defines itself in relation to itself considered as not-art. If the photographs are redundant, it is only because, in the end, they point out the redundancy, and uselessness, of art. Art is so preciously in this world, so worth holding onto, so important, because it is not in service of something else. For, although the photographs and the piazza invite us to contemplate the shrapnel scars, it is the photographs in particular which ask us to re-view the shrapnel damage as beautiful. They have the demonstrative *there it is* function, which Barthes attributes to photography. They frame the scars, drawing our attention to them, reducing them literally to surface. They allow us to view the scars much closer than we could normally get to them, where we can fall into their elusive coloured universe. Their *intergalacticity* only becomes apparent after the photographs.

The real transgression is not that we are asked to aestheticise the war, but that we are asked to assent to the suggestion that the photograph is instrumental in transforming these scars into works of art. Usually when you take a photograph, the photograph becomes art, not its object. Here the camera is an art-gun: you aim it at something, pull the trigger, flash of light and hey presto: art! We could propose research into exactly how it works, its theoretical consequences, and what subject matter it works on. A look at how publications have been instrumental in elevating certain buildings to the status of architectural icons, suggests that this speculation

6. "...the severe exclusion of meretricious decoration..." (commentary on the proposal in 1893). In 1941, the Luftwaffe sent a more energetic critique.
Tate Archives, *South Elevation on 23 September 1941*

is convincing for buildings. Ditto for the food portrait by which classy cookbooks have promoted cuisine as a formal art. It puts a new spin on the idea of the art photographer. The art gun is an extreme extension of Malraux's museum without walls, according to which the museum will be replaced by the photograph book as collector and storage container for art.[19] Most of the objects in Malraux's photograph collection were already art – already in the museum – and his project was about getting rid of the museum.[20]

These inscriptions may be closer to automatic photography than to automatic writing. Automatic photography is a disinterested photography, the instances or authors of which I am not familiar. It has to do with photographing what you do not care about, or do not want, or do not value, such as miscellaneous shrapnel damage. It is the opposite – and yet almost identical to – the tourist snapshot, which attempts to capture something you value highly, but which always necessarily eludes you. It is close to – and yet could not be farther from – throwing the camera into the air with the shutter on a one-second delay, which will always only ever capture the utterly meaningless.

These arguments point towards thinking architecture not as body, but as machine. The redundancy of these photographs derives from the possibility of identifying them with their object, the building itself; and therefore thinking the building as a completely alien thing. The redundancy is thus symptomatic of a break in the anthropocentric link that has operated in architecture, and has motivated architectural discourse since the Renaissance, and via the Renaissance, since Vitruvius, when monuments and livers where both surfaces for inscription. Against

7. Maimed buildings
E. Ruff, *Arras, the town hall after the bombardment, 15 December 1915*

this, we posit the building which does not make meaning the way a body does: through Latin inscriptions upon its surface, the superimposition of a geometry upon the prone body, or through the divination of livers, unless this divination is rethought as a flash of light – an insight from God – from some completely alien place. The building becomes the indifferent plate to a flash of light. The building means the way a photograph means, as a record, an imprint, as if by a flash of light, which distances itself irrevocably from human agency. The camera is the only machine which produces meaning by itself. The typewriter or its replacement, MicrosoftWord™, are only tools for producing meaning by an operator, (and everybody knows that automatic drawing is a bit of a hoax). A consequence of this identity is that architecture and the photograph may begin to replace each other, or interact with each other in intense ways which call into question their heretofore inviolate status, as in the photo-*realist* work of Pierre Vivant.

   This paper was predicated on the identity of architecture and body, an identity which even Le Cor-*house-is-a-machine-for-living-in*-busier subscribed to. It has been fuelled by the seemingly radical – but ultimately predictable – desire to place a photograph of Arras and a photograph of Roehampton together and say they are the same. This paper now ends with the thought that architecture does not make meaning by the hand of man, by inscription, but by the flash of light, which comes from the outside, and rains down on man and beast and rock of the earth equally.

NOTES

1 See for example, E. Ruff, *Guerre Européenne: Arras Bombardé*, E. Le Deley, Paris, n.d. but probably before the end of World War I), which has the cheerful decorative format of a tourist guide.

2 Brian Brice Taylor, *Le Corbusier at Pessac*, Fondation Le Corbusier, Paris, 1972.

3 We broaden the field to include the stoppages of Duchamp and the action paintings of Jackson Pollock, and any other practice which eschews authorial intention and meaning, and chooses instead to accuse the surface. Even in the work of realist painters like Thomas Eakins, surface inscription intrudes from the outside to disfigure the stated intentions of the work. See for example, Michael Fried, *Realism Writing and Disfiguration*, for a discussion of the traces of perspective construction in Eakins' illusionistic canvases. In architecture, the façade would have imposed the necessary unifying…

8 "Nouvel at the Beaubourg", extracts from a lecture at the Centre Georges Pompidou, January 1992, published in Iwona, Blazwick, et al., eds., *Nouvel* , Artemis, Arc-en-Rêve, ICA, London and Zurich, 1992, pp. 120-122.

9 Ibid., p. 122.

10 Gilles Deleuze, *The Logic of Sense*, Transl. by Mark Lester, Athlone Press, London, 1990. See in particular "Second Series of Paradoxes of Surface Effects", pp. 4-11.

11 Ibid., p4.

12 An opposition which Adolf Loos presupposed in "Ornament and Crime", where he likened ornament to what he saw to be the inessential body decorations of (ignoble) savages.

13 Quoted from LeCorbusier, *Towards a New Architecture*. Translated by F. Etchells.

14 The most comprehensive discussion of listing occurs in "The Modern Cult of Monuments", in which Alois Riegl defines the values of artefacts for the *Kunstwollen*. Riegl accepts that any argument for the preservation of an artefact – ancient monument or contemporary art – has to be framed in terms of its value to contemporary sensibility. Riegl reads like an *avant la lettre* Teutonic Deleuzian, for his idea of value is close to the idea of

the event-inscribed surface. For monuments of the past, he distinguishes historical-value from age-value. A monument accrues value because it represents a moment of the past based upon when it was built, or it accrues value purely because it is old. Artefacts accrue age value because of the ravages of time and war since "additions by human hands assume over time the appearance of natural forces". They become valuable not because they issue from an historic event, but because they bear the wearing and tearing marks of time. Historic value and age value are obviously related, since something will not be historical without being old, but they are also in conflict because monuments only retain their historical value to the extent that they are not allowed to deteriorate beyond recognition. Age value is in direct conflict with art-value, and, in particular, a subspecies of art-value called newness-value, according to which artefacts are valued because of their "integrity of form and colour", which is most manifest when they are new. The restoration of historic

monuments "rests essentially on the two premises of the originality of style (its historical-value) and the unity of style (its newness-value)". Listing grafts age value and historic value, by preserving war damage and giving it the historic status of an event. See Alois Riegl, "The Modern Cult of Monuments: Its Character and Its Origin", transl. by Kurt Forster and Diane Ghirardo, in *Oppositions 25*, Rizzoli, New York, Fall 1982. Originally published in Riegl, *Gessammelte Aufsätze*, Vienna, 1928.

15 John Hershey, *Hiroshima*.

16 Deleuze, p. 5.

17 Roland Barthes, *Camera Lucida: Reflections on Photography*, Transl. by Richard Howard, Hill & Wang, New York, 1981, pp. 26-27.

18 Deleuze, pp. 8-9.

19 Andre Malraux, *The Voices of Silence*, Princeton University Press, Princeton, 1978.

20 Douglas Crimp sees Malraux's project as making explicit a crisis for modern art to the extent at least that it is an institutionalised practice. Every museum presupposes a principle for collecting; it becomes the principle of unity of

121

art. Modern art has put the museum in crisis, because it problematises these boundaries. According to Crimp, in Malraux's hands, the photograph becomes the only possible principle of unity upon which the museum collection is based. This breaks down when the collection includes photographs of photographs. The present case is even more perverse, because the photograph claims to generate art, not merely display it, and the subject of the photographs is the museum itself. See Douglas Crimp, "On The Museum's Ruins" in Hal Foster, ed., *The Anti-Aesthetic*, Bay Press, Port Townsend, WA., 1983. Derrida returns to this problem in his discussion of framing in Kant's *Critique of Judgement* in "Parergon". See Jacques Derrida, *The Truth in Painting*, University of Chicago Press, Chicago, 1987.

1989. Reprinted by permission of Red Cross Society Archives.

2   William S. Rubin, *Dada and Surrealist Art*, Abrams, New York, n.d. Reprinted by permission of the Museum of Modern Art, New York.

3   Houk Randall and Ted Polhemus, *The Customized Body*, Serpent's Tail, London, 1996.

4   James Wellard, *The Search for the Etruscians*, Nelson Publishing, London, 1973.

5   Pierre Vivant, *En Passant, Residencies 1991-92*, Pierre Vivant, Southhampton, 1993.

6   Frances Spalding, *The Tate: A History*, Tate Gallery Pulbishing, London, 1998.

7   E. Ruff, *Guerre Européene: Arras Bombarde*, E. Le Deley, Paris, n.d.

IMAGE CREDITS

Images of shrapnel damage by Lorens Holm.

Other images:

1   Jane Carmichael, *First World War Photographers,* Routledge, New York,

THE FLICKER (1966)

TRAVIS MILES

125

In 1966, a year that was arguably the apogee of the American
'Underground' avant-garde film scene, Tony Conrad's *The Flicker* was
screened at the New York Film Festival. Composed only of black and
white (clear) frame alternations, *The Flicker* was presented with warning
titles indicating that it might cause epileptic seizures in a minute
percentage of the audience and that a physician should be at hand during
the screening. Although none of the audience (then or to date) displayed
epileptic tendencies, the film *did* manage to cause headaches or mild
hallucinations in some observers. According to Conrad, "After the
premiére screening at the New York Film-Makers' Cinemathèque, the guy
who ran the theater told me a week later he still had a splitting headache."[1]

Conrad first conceived of the project after attending a class on the
physiology of the nervous system at Harvard, where he graduated with a
degree in Mathematics in 1962. Not surprisingly, Conrad's subsequent
creative work has been heavily inflected by his training in the analytical
sciences, marked by tremendous mathematical precision and a rigorous
adherence to progressive experimentation. *The Flicker* itself is based on a

formal series of alternations designed to gradually expose the viewer to dynamic stroboscopic effects before phasing them out at the same rate. As Conrad learned from his physiology class:

> the range of perception of flicker or stroboscopic light is below a frequency of about 40 flashes per second (40 fps), above which the light is seen as continuous. Normal sound projection is at 24 fps. Below 24 fps, the only real effect is of the light switching on and off. But in the range from 6 to 18 fps, more or less, strange things occur. *The Flicker* moves gradually from 24 fps to 4 fps and then back out of the flicker range again.[2]

Conrad structured the film into 47 patterns of alternation (white/black), based on his notion of visual 'harmonic frequency relationships'.[3] If human perception of flicker effect principally occurs between 4 and 40 fps, and each of these flashes per second is treated as equivalent to a note in auditory harmonic relationships, then flicker 'harmonies' may be established over a range of up to three octaves (12 'notes' each). Since standard film projection operates at 24 frames per second, however, harmonic relationships in *filmed* flicker must be established between 4 and 24 frames per second or approximately 1 and 1/2 octaves.

The patterns at the beginning and end of the film reflect each other, representing the path into and out of the dense middle section: "Each numerical progression dominates a given section of variable length of the film: 23 clear, 1 black, then 11 clear, 1 black, 9/1, 8/1, 7/1, 6/1, 5/1, 2/1, 1/1 and then back out again, the reversal of the pattern ending again with 23/1."[4] Within the middle section bracketed by these patterns, Conrad allows for non-progressive variations designed to explore his concept of stroboscopic harmonics between the rates of 6 and 18 fps. Patterns in this middle section may therefore appear erratic or irregular, as in groupings of 5/1-4/1-5/1 changes. The film's overall construction brings to mind procedures of hypnotic therapy, proceeding from induction to hypnosis to withdrawal.

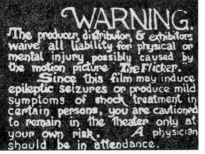

Before 'shooting' the initial 4,000 frames of film from which he processed a further 40,000 frames in the lab, Conrad mapped out the exact exposures which he required on a timing matrix. Extant photographs of this matrix confirm the immense complexity involved in establishing harmonic patterns as well as the plastic beauty of its composition.

The matrix is difficult to interpret, especially as it is not clear if it is to be read horizontally or vertically. Nevertheless, photographs clearly show the spatial dynamics implicit in Conrad's arrangement; the density of the interior section and the gradual, almost rounded, phasing in/out of the extended patterns at the matrix edge. Graphically, the patterns have the appearance of an explosion, successive waves emanating from an indeterminate epicentre. Its pixillated roughness when viewed from a distance visually evokes the early filmic experiments with computer-generated imagery that it immediately precedes.[5] Additionally, the expanding spiral pattern brings to mind the attempts of Jordan Belson and other West-coast filmmakers to produce transcendental experiences in the viewer through the use of abstract or 'Eastern-mystical' imagery. Finally, in its alternation of black and white marks, its mathematical patterns based on harmonics, and its reduction of a temporal event to a graphic representation, the matrix also strongly resembles the score of a musical composition. As I will make clear later, these evocations result to a great extant from Conrad's somewhat remarkable position at the confluence of several avant-garde trends.

The effects of the film, as mentioned above, vary from hallucinations to headaches, with one in 15,000 adults potentially suffering the onset of photogenic migraine or epileptic fit. Programme notes for the film (as in the NY Film-Makers' Cooperative catalogue), as well as the small body of critical literature surrounding it, describe audience perceptions of colours, objects, and concentric circles generated from the black/white alternation. The most common perception, according to Conrad, was that of

127

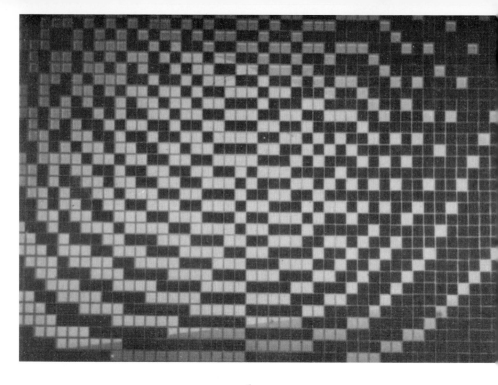

"colored, jiggling mandala-type figures."[6] In contrast, those audience members who were "apprehensive or anxious" (i.e. not receptive), tended to see nothing unusual or to develop tense headaches.

TONY CONRAD BEFORE 1966

In 1966, despite being included in the New York Film Festival programme, *The Flicker* remained at the venue where it had debuted the year before, a small theatre called the Film-Makers' Cinémathèque. The New York Film-Makers' Cooperative had established the Film-Makers' Cinémathèque in 1964 after police curtailed screenings at the Charles Theater in the Lower East Side. The purpose of the Cinémathèque was to provide an exhibition space for the work of Cooperative members, and as such tended to derive its audience from these filmmakers and hangers-on.

The Film-Makers' Cooperative was the epicentre of what was then known as the 'Underground' film movement in the United States, although this term was hotly contested or disliked by a good deal of the artists concerned. Administrated by filmmaker Jonas Mekas, the Cooperative in 1966 had reached the peak of its notoriety. Jack Smith's

Flaming Creatures (1962-63), which contained male/female nudity as well as transvestism and homosexual material, had been labelled obscene by New York courts and was refused exhibition at the 1963 Knokke-Le Zoute festival in Belgium. Since the film had been partially produced through the Cooperative, Mekas used the scandal to proclaim the contrary virtues of the underground movement, even projecting the film into the face of the Belgian Minister of Justice at Knokke-Le Zoute. The avant-garde films emerging from this scene were thus generally perceived as primarily a challenge to *social* mores and thereby deserving of the appellation 'Underground', with its attendant connotations of moral aberrance and institutional suppression.

    The key films of this movement had indeed contained material or images that at that time were considered counter-cultural.[7] Moreover, these films were seen as illicit, due to the low-gauge technology employed, technology that had previously been associated almost exclusively with home-filmmaking. This association lent underground films an air of perverse voyeurism, as if viewers were privy to what should be the private activities of the filmmaker. Predominant forms included the film diary (Mekas, Taylor Mead), subjective 'film-essays' (Stan Brakhage, Gregory Markopoulos), presentations of bizarre tableaux or personalities (Ron Rice, Jack Smith, Andy Warhol), and *détournements* of popular imagery (Kenneth Anger, Bruce Connor). Posed against the industrial practice of Hollywood and the European New Waves, underground film was a predominantly subjective and expressive practice, summed up by the subtitle of Stan Brakhage's 1961 film *Films By Stan Brakhage: An Avant-Garde Home Movie.*[8]

    Proponents of the underground movement saw this focus on subjective experience as the inauguration of a cinema of poetry, while others saw at it as hopelessly mired in an outdated (read 'bourgeois') conception of art practice. Jean-Luc Godard, reflecting on the American movement through his script for the Dziga Vertov Group's 1972 film *Wind from the East,* stated that the underground constitutes "a cinema which thinks it is liberated. A drug cinema. A sex cinema. A cinema which claims it has been liberated by poetry, art. A cinema with no taboos, except the class struggle."[9]

Conrad had been associated with the underground scene since late 1962, collaborating on or appearing in films by Jonas Mekas and Ron Rice as well as providing soundtrack material for Jack Smith's *Flaming Creatures* (1962-63) and *Normal Love* (unfinished, 1963-).[10] It was, in fact, as a musician that Conrad had made his entrance into New York avant-garde circles. While still at Harvard, Conrad became increasingly interested in contemporary composition, largely due to a John Cage/David Tudor performance he attended in Boston in 1959. Also in 1959, Conrad met the future Minimalist composer LaMonte Young, whom Conrad sought out upon his arrival in New York City in 1962.

MINIMALIST COMPOSITION

Young was to prove both a tremendous influence and hindrance to Conrad's career, providing him with an introduction to the compositional practice that would establish his name in experimental music, yet denying Conrad's reciprocal contribution in subsequent accounts of their work together. According to Conrad, he began to sit in at Young's Theatre of Eternal Music in 1962, where the composer and a group of others carried on almost constant experiments in alternative modes of performance and instrumentality.[11] All of the instruments used were tuned in just intonation, a tuning based on whole number ratios between harmonic intervals, rather than the standard method of tuning by half or quarter steps.

Conrad, a trained violinist, claims to have played a single note for the first month of his involvement with the group, only later adding another, an open fifth, to produce intervallic (rather than harmonic) variation. The style of music preferred by the Theatre involved sustained drones, produced via voice (Young and Zazeela), amplified strings (Conrad, Cale), and hand drums (MacLise). Variation and tempo were kept to a minimum in order that each tone might be explored and exposed in full, often for a period of several hours. As such, these experiments are perceived as the inception of Minimalist compositional practice in the United States, with Young as its most influential (and infamous) practitioner. After the group drifted apart in 1965, Young consistently down-played the contributions of all Theatre members besides himself, even going so far as to refuse access to the myriad rehearsal-recordings generated between 1962 and 1965.[12]

For Conrad, the genius of the Theatre had primarily involved a three-fold avant-garde practice enacted at the levels of composition, appropriation, and performance, all of which would later influence his filmmaking. In terms of composition, the *Dream Music* which the group produced erased the separation between composer and performer, construction and process. "As a response to the un-choices of the composer Cage, here were composerly choices that were specified to a completeness that included and concluded the performance itself."[13] In this scheme, the composer as such was imbedded in the process, rather than at some remove from it. Compositional choices were to be made from 'inside' the work and emphasise its mutability.

This compositional practice became pivotal to the establishment of Minimalist aesthetics in the United States, due to its complete focus on the constituent elements of its medium. As Conrad notes, Minimalism was "the serious discovery on the part of the artists that by confining their tools and concerns more narrowly than had ever been proposed, they could achieve wider understandings and more profound circumstances for the reception of their work."[14] Minor fluctuations in pitch and tone, as well as the intervallic relationships between tones, displaced melody and expression as the central concerns of composition. Paradoxically, as choices were reduced to almost binary alternations, this reduction resulted in the extreme magnification of previously insignificant shifts.

Young and Conrad, like many musicians of the early sixties, were profoundly effected by the non-Western music that was then becoming available in the United States.[15] Conrad heard in this music, specifically North-Indian Classical styles, an established and rich tradition based on the same principles which the Theatre was attempting to explore: namely "the drone, which expanded attentiveness to intervallic relations while eliminating the function of harmonic motion."[16] *Dream Music* was in part an appropriation of this tradition, done so in the hope of extending its implications into a new musical language by combining it with a specifically Western avant-garde project. From the first, then, Conrad and Young's musical project explicitly engaged non-Western aesthetic forms while transforming them through theoretical, mathematically precise strategies.

The Theatre represented a performance practice and use of performance space in direct opposition to the established practices of the New York 'high-cultural' scene at that time. *Dream Music* performances could last for the majority of a day or only a few hours, were never publicised and seldom attended for their entire duration. Conrad viewed the group's activities as part and parcel of a larger counter-cultural movement that included other New York movements like Fluxus, the Andy Warhol/Factory scene, and the 'Underground Movie' scene, which, for Conrad, "reconstructed the movies as a documentary form – a merging of life – aims with movie production."[17] Alongside Henry Flynt, a future member of the Fluxus group, Conrad had been picketing New York museums and high-culture performance spaces since 1963, "in opposition to the imperialist influences of European high culture."[18] The dissolution of the Theatre in 1965 led Conrad to locate other outlets for his on-going experiments in counter-cultural, intervallic, aesthetic forms.

CONRAD S FILM PRACTICE

With *The Flicker*, Conrad extended the work he had done with the Theatre into the underground film milieu. *The Flicker* replicates the three-fold avant-garde practice which Conrad had seen at work in the *Dream Music*, re-situating it to suit the demands of the medium. At first glance, the compositional practice described by Conrad in relation to the *Dream Music* and that which he employed to construct *The Flicker* appear somewhat divergent. *Dream Music* composition was not separate from performance process, whereas *The Flicker* was strictly mapped prior to its execution and was, in fact, produced from the equivalent of a musical 'score'; the matrix described above. However, given Conrad's dedication to the exploration of intervallic relationships and to the minimalist focus on constituent materials, the two practices may be reconciled.

The Flicker addresses film composition at its most basic level, the alternation of white (light) and black (no-light). All film is composed of varying degrees of light and shadow, just as all film produces stroboscopic effect. By stripping the film of objective imagery, Conrad is able to foreground the inherent flickering which otherwise would go unnoticed, or which would be subsumed by continuity between successive images. This mimics the Theatre's decision to foreground intonation and duration over and above melody or expressivity. Just as compositional work was conducted inside *Dream Music* rather than prior to or external to it, Conrad expected the effects of *The Flicker* to vary widely from viewer to viewer, depending on their attitude to the material and their predisposition to meditative or hallucinatory experiences.

In this sense, the filmic experience is, to a much greater extent than in the case of presentations of objective imagery, determined by the viewer. Conrad's overtly mathematical formula for the film is no more than a sort of tuning, similar to the just intonation chosen by the Theatre participants. He introduces "light patterns which are related harmonically to the drone of the normal projection frequency",[19] but images or effects derived from these patterns depend on the compositional choices and disposition of the viewer.

One of the effects which Conrad was most interested in was meditative or hypnotic tendencies provoked by the variations of the film's middle section. Abstract photographic imagery, as well as images generated by experimental animation techniques, have been known to produce mild trance-like states in viewers. Within the avant-garde, various filmmakers had attempted to induce meditative states, often with explicitly Eastern mystical imagery. James Whitney's *Yantra* (1955) involved hand-drawn mandalas, composed of thousands of dots, which expanded, contracted, and divided to form a multitude of shapes.

Experimentation with meditative effect based on objective imagery reached its apex with Jordan Belson, a West-coast filmmaker who had

abandoned film in the early sixties to study Hatha Yoga. Returning to film in 1964, Belson's subsequent films all involved mandalic imagery based on his understanding of tantric philosophy. David James describes Belson's work as "a film practice in which kinaesthetic optical effects are both produced in response to the visual and visionary experience of altered states of consciousness and used to achieve them."[20] Conrad's film, while not derived from any specific non-Western philosophy, was based on altering perception without the use of any imagery whatsoever. As he states, "I was convinced art was about changing how people think."[21]

Belson and Conrad, however, would have radically different notions of the quality and meaning of meditative states once these states were produced by visual stimuli. For Belson, meditation was inseparable from religious practice, and as such his films were principally devotional works intended to sacralise the medium. Conrad intended the meditational effects of his film to contribute to the larger project of Minimalism, that is, to inspire reflection on the constituent elements of the medium and the way in which they could be manipulated. Meditation for Conrad was not a path out of the visual experience and into transcendent thought. On

the contrary, meditation was to be a meditation *on the medium itself*,
reflecting the materialist, avant-garde practice which the Theatre of
Eternal Music had derived from non-Western idioms.

> Encouraging the audience in a meditative direction was a way of creating
> an atmosphere of sacred expectations that was achieved in the gallery or
> museum through the imposition of the white cube and the silent
> treatment. The way reflection could be understood and made legible in
> that day was to carry over audience expectations based on the drug
> experience and on meditational experiences.[22]

WHITE OF THE EYE

The Flicker carries out a complex programme of de-mystification through
the shoring up of contemporary art-exhibition practices. The 'atmosphere
of sacred expectations', utilised by galleries and museums to simulate a
ritualistic or cultic attitude to aesthetic objects, is converted by Conrad
into reflection on the material conditions of exhibition. The white light
produced by the projector when passing through the clear frames of *The
Flicker* illuminates both the screen and the audience itself, exposing both
as components of a specific performance environment. The viewer's
attention is drawn to the fact that they are watching only the play of light
on a white screen, while the source of light (the projector) is revealed as
the primary filmic apparatus over and above the camera or the film.

Conrad's exposure of the projector's centrality pre-figures the
developments of artists who would later come under the heading of
'expanded cinema', that is, conceptual work that took film performance
and exhibition as its subject. Prior to *The Flicker*, Conrad and Jack Smith
had explored stroboscopic effects using only projector light. Smith
himself tended to incorporate film into larger performative events which

could include all manner of theatrical 'violations' of standard viewing experiences. A frequent collaborator of Smith's, Ken Jacobs, put on shows that "mimicked with live shadows the appearance of a film."[23] Other projector-centred works include Nam June Paik's *Zen for Film* (a ten-minute strip of clear celluloid run through the projector) and the activities of Takehisa Kosugi, who ran the projector without film in it at all. Both Paik and Kosugi were directly engaged with movements that had influenced Conrad; Paik was then a burgeoning video-artist associated with the Fluxus group, while Kosugi, also associated with Fluxus, would follow John Cage as resident composer for the Merce Cunningham Dance Company.

While *The Flicker* may have contributed to the genesis of 'expanded cinema' due to its deliberate foregrounding of the projector and the exhibition environment, its Minimalist focus on film's basic material units pointed in an entirely different direction. So-called 'structural' filmmaking began to emerge in 1966 and set to work producing films "in which this or that single element in the total register of the codes of filmic signification has been isolated, set into lonely self-display."[24] This sort of filmmaking quickly overtook the older underground, which had been based more on a subjective appropriation of the medium than a rigorous exploration of film form.[25] The filmmakers who came to prominence as 'structural' or 'materialist' practitioners tended to be outsiders of the New York scene, although there were some cross-overs. Conrad himself occupies a unique position in regards to these movements, as he appears firmly planted in each: a filmmaker interested in generating subjective experience precisely *through* a materialist Minimalism.[26]

Conrad's choice of black and white alternation is central to this paradox. By limiting all visual information to black and white frames, the film also predetermines the viewer's response as reaction/anticipation. White light comes to stand in for action, dialogue, mise-en-scène; i.e., what is *present* as the content of most films. Rather than merely emphasising the projector, *The Flicker* exposes the basic ontological premise of film. Projected film is an even split between darkness and light, as the light source is obscured by shutters as often as it is open. Within its unique domain, the film claims white is *what is*, while black is *what is not*.

Positing whiteness as immanence was directly opposed to the view held by galleries and exhibition spaces of the sixties which held that white was an absolute neutrality against which art could stand out as pure enunciation. In *The Flicker*, however, it is whiteness that is the basic unit of expression, and not merely expression but of *presence* itself. Pushed back to its structural limit, the film can only pulse its Morse-like composition as evidence of it being a human construction. This composition, Conrad implies, is the slightest and most beautiful way of harnessing what is the source and necessity of all film: white light.

Of course, *The Flicker* cannot be said to be *about* anything outside its intentional variation of stroboscopic effects. As I have shown, however, the film carries within it the conflict between expressive composition and the attempt to dislocate conventional associations through an application of minimalist practice. Conrad, through his activities with the Theatre of Eternal Music and with the underground film scene, struggled to wed his reductive aesthetics to art forms which remained expressive, and which would be sacralised by this austere formalism. The projector's white light was for Conrad the limit of this austerity, and its hypnotic variation the purest and most basic composition within that medium (hence, for Minimalism, the most beautiful).

> Although today we tend to look back and discount some of these seemingly 'spiritual' elements as artistic chaff, in effect, that's a discrimination which is made unevenly. It is allowed to condemn the idealism of New Age thinking but not of the Civil Rights movement, and is allowed to condemn the hubris of the anti-war movement but not of the gallery or museum...[27]

NOTES

1 Tony Conrad interviewed by Mark Bloch, April 15, 1998 at http://archive.abcnews.go.com/sections/world/DailyNews/flicker_conrad.html.

2 From a letter to Henry Romney, dated November 11, 1965 and published in *Film Culture*, No. 41, 1966. Reprinted in Robert Russett and Cecile Starr, *Experimental Animation: Origins of a New Art*, Revised Edition, Da Capo, New York, 1976, p. 152.

3 Ibid., p. 153.

4 Maureen Cheryn Turim, *Abstraction in Avant-Garde Films*, UMI Research Press, Ann Arbor, 1985, p. 98.

5 Conrad's 'day-job' prior to receiving a Rockefeller grant in 1965 was as a computer programmer.

6 Tony Conrad interviewed by Mark Bloch, April 15, 1998 at http://archive.abcnews.go.com/sections/world/DailyNews/flicker_conrad.html

7 A list of such 'key' films would of course vary from individual to individual, yet I propose that a select group may nonetheless be singled out from this pre-1966 period: Jack Smith's *Flaming Creatures* (1962-63), Kenneth Anger's *Scorpio Rising* (1963), Ken Jacobs' *Blonde Cobra* (1959-63), Stan Brakhage's *Dog Star Man* (1961-64), Ron Rice's *Chumlum* (1964), and Gregory Markopoulos' *Twice a Man* (1962-63).

8 Significantly, Brakhage's film plays with the conception of underground film as voyeuristic by presenting images of him and his wife making love superimposed with footage of their children, effectively combining aesthetic and social transgressions.

9 Jean-Luc Godard, *Weekend/Wind from the East*, Simon and Schuster, New York, 1972, p. 164.

10 In addition to these personal connections to the underground, Conrad was married to actress Beverly Grant, who appeared in several underground films before collaborating with Conrad himself on various film projects in the early seventies.

11 This group included, at various times, the visual artist Marian Zazeela (Young's wife), musician John Cale, and composer/musician Angus MacLise.

12 Young released copies of the tapes to Conrad and Cale in 1990 on the

condition that they sign an agreement stating that he, LaMonte Young, was the sole 'composer' of the 'pieces'. This agreement utterly contradicts Young's compositional philosophy of the sixties, while exemplifying Young's notorious self-aggrandising tactics.

13 Tony Conrad, *Lyssophobia: On Four Violins*, published at www.tonyconrad.com/main.html.

14 Chris Hill, 1995 interview with Tony Conrad published at www.nomadnet.org/massage/video/page8.html.

15 Conrad states: "The first recording of Indian music I heard was an Ali Akbar Khan performance on Angel Records, in late 1959. It was electrifying, my recollection is vivid." Tony Conrad, *Lyssophobia: On Four Violins*, published at www.tonyconrad.com/main.html.

16 Ibid.

17 Ibid.

18 Ibid.

19 Tony Conrad interviewed by Mark Bloch, April 15, 1998 at http://archive.abcnews.go.com/sections/world/DailyNews/flicker_conrad.html.

20 David E. James, *Allegories of Cinema: American Film in the Sixties*, Princeton University Press, Princeton, 1989, p. 128.

21 Tony Conrad interviewed by Mark Bloch, April 15, 1998 at http://archive.abcnews.go.com/sections/world/DailyNews/flicker_conrad.html.

22 Chris Hill, 1995 interview with Tony Conrad published at URL:http://www.nomadnet.org/massage/video/page8.html.

23 Sheldon Renan, *The Underground Film: An Introduction to its Development in America*, Studio Vista, London, 1968, p. 33.

24 David E. James, *Allegories of Cinema: American Film in the Sixties*, Princeton University Press, Princeton, 1989, p. 242.

26 As does Ken Jacobs, who had worked with Jack Smith, Conrad, and Jonas Mekas.

27 Chris Hill, 1995 interview with Tony Conrad published at URL: http://www.nomadnet.org/massage/video/page8.html.

IMAGE CREDITS

Both images are reprinted from Stephen Dwoskin, *Film is...the international free cinema*, Peter Owen Ltd., London, 1975.

WHITENESS

METAL MACHINE MUSIC

SURFACE EFFECT OF SOUND AND IDENTITY IN THE DIGITAL AGE

CHRISTOPHER HIGHT

PRE-FACE, OR SHUT YOUR MOUTH

A camera pulls slowly back from a man's face. He is strutting – in time with the soundtrack – down an urban boulevard. Eventually the camera reveals a musical entourage, playing the pastiched Isaac Hays groove that motivates his movement. The wah-wah guitars and staccato horn coalesce into a compulsive image, providing the character's genetic (*stereo*) type. The super hero of the ghetto, he is Shaft or Sam Spade. Without context or narrative, these sounds tell us that this "cat's a bad mother…"[1]

This audio-visual gag from the film *I'm Going to Get You Sucka!* works by parodic intensification, that is, by short-circuiting a habitual assemblage of sound and vision, revealing its tautological absurdity. But towards what is our guffaw directed? Besides the usual suspects (ourselves, Hollywood) there exists another, altogether more elusive, target. Just as the camera zooms from a close-up to reveal the context in which the punch-line emerges, this acoustic image ef-faces our bodies, black and white, with a surface effect, a façade, a face. We find at this intersection of hilarity and disgust the sheer face of whiteness.

This face is not a literal skin (black or white), nor any specific or stereotyped caricature, but a conceptual radical superficiality. It does not encode a meaning but induces effects (laughter, screams); this acoustic image operates as what Deleuze and Guattari have named, "the abstract machine of faciality (*visagéité*)".[3] Faciality is *abstract* in that it operates on an immanent yet pre-conscious, pre-representational level (Deleuze's 'virtual'). Psychically prior to the mirror-stage, as if the silvered substrate of reflectivity, it differentiates the "gazeless eyes" of a "body without organs".[4] Faciality is *machinic* in that it actuates these unformed virtualities into concretised concepts. It diagrammatically constructs a 'black hole/ white wall system' of signification and subjectification, drawing power not from a sovereign subject, inalienable rights, nor natural categories but from a creative will (to power) and force itself. For this reason, 'the face is not universal', *a priori*, or general, but an onto-aesthetical framework within which judgement can only be prejudicial, orientated, as it were, according to the epistemology faciality inscribes. It does not represent a given subject, but fabricates molar identification (race, sex, philosopher). Indeed, in as much as it is white, "it is not even that of the white man; it is White Man himself, with his broad white cheeks and the black holes of

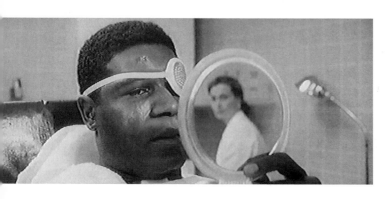

Clay not seeing himself not seeing himself

his eyes".[5] In other words, it is that which allows the concept of the White Man to come forth and freeze the world according to its order of things. This abstract machine operates at a preconscious, pre-significatory moment – it is only through its conceptual fabrications that the face becomes sensible as a sign and a site of domination. Keeping in mind the triple connotation of the French *blanc* as white, white hot (*blanche*) and blank or empty, the white face (*le visage blanc*) is a substrate of language, a semiotic rather than a semiosis. Like an empty musical staff ready for inscription, or the empty lectern upon which an orator will stand. This faciality is thus the cruel joke of racist absurdity: the white wall as the abstract significatory plane upon which other bodies are coded, the black hole (eye's and mouth) the machine of despotic subjectification. Before the colonial gaze, there was the construction of the binocular portals of whiteness, the black hole sockets in which signification is captured.

The task – and the source – of our laughter is then *not* one of unmasking whiteness, nor does it repress content, but rather it is an enunciation, amplified and modulated in order to disrupt the machinations of faciality. Exfoliating the preconscious conditions of faciality is not a matter of *looking* in depth, of finding a hidden meaning, a cause, a part object, a fragmented truth, an orginary signifier. Similarly, phenomenology always find its stoppage at the wall of faciality by predicting 'the body' as the threshold of interior/exterior, subject/object when the abstract machine of faciality installs the concept of the body, the perceptual primacy. These quests for a signified cause treat the face as a sign, the body as cause, rather than addressing faciality as an envelope of *incorporeal*, but nevertheless *real*, forces. On the other hand, parody acknowledges the power of these signs as a complex site in and of itself, as cusps and catastrophic pleats in the radical superficiality of faciality. It does not deny signification, but by intensifying acoustic-image of the sign itself to hyperbole, it reconfigures and redirects its force.

Moreover, our scene's parodic force suggests how insidiously image and noise collude in delineating the pre-conscious face of race and of racism, the representational surface upon which 'whiteness' has spread to cover the modern sensory landscape. Taking the parody as a cue, this essay seeks to map this mannered, frozen countenance – that is, the White Face – by examining a few intersections of sound and vision. One peculiar film, *Suture*, and Ralph Ellison's *Invisible Man* serve as audio-visual case studies into depths of superficiality. Or rather, they are *sampled*, in a movement from the traditional visual-spatial tropes of racism towards the sonic-temporal mechanisms of faciality in part suggested by Jacques Attali's political economy of music. Re-mixing the story of racism as the soundtrack of whiteness at once fleshes out Deleuze and Guattari's concept of faciality while problematising their gloss. More importantly, these sonic excursions into the territory of the White Face attempt to locate a-synchronisms in this white noise, in which new modes of productive resistance may begin their improvisation. Only through the *dépaysément* of the sign as acoustic-image with preconscious associative affects can one confront the regime of faciality. If this bleached façade, this *blanc visage* of whiteness, cannot be bored through to reveal a more fundamental truth or exploded into infinite interpretations, it can be scaled by mapping the folds and involutions of its features.

white light   a condition of illumination composed of an even distribution of frequencies within the visible spectrum.[6]

The film *Suture* continually juxtaposes music with electronic noises. The sound from a touch-tone phone detonates a near-lethal car bomb; a plastic surgeon reconstructs the victim's face while listening to a Wagner aria over cacophonous equipment noise. And it is through this sonic shock-wave of an explosion and its juxtaposition with music that the film fully actuates its conceit.[7]

This film *blanc* (as the directors called it, noting its narrative similarity and formal differentiation from film noir) sets up a cinematic paradox: the narrative of the plot and character's speech does not match their associated images. A plot summary is indistinguishable from any pulp story of reversal and betrayal. In unspecified trouble, Vincent attempts to murder his look-alike brother, Clay, to appear it is he who was killed and thus allowing escape to a new life. Clay lives, however, and has complete amnesia. Clay undergoes extensive plastic surgery, which reconstructs his shattered face according to a picture of his brother, as a therapist similarly attempts to reconstruct his forgotten identity in the belief that he is Vincent. Effectively re-made into his brothers' image, Clay assumes his brother's identity, falling in love with his plastic surgeon. Vincent then returns to finish the job, but Clay literally blows his face off with a shotgun. The violence of the event jars Clay's memory, but he decides to continue living as Vincent. This sub-Hitchockian story line is rather predictable, though it plays with the genre's clichés with a clever glee.

But the film's effect stems not from its narrative, but from a formal reification, expressed by its exceedingly clinical photography and most importantly through uniquely high-concept casting 'against type'. The characters are intentionally ciphers for this conceit. However many times the narrative tells us Clay and Vincent are doubles, that Clay has been remade into the image of Vincent, the actors cast to play these parts are nothing alike. 'Vincent' is a small pinched, smooth operator ensconced in fine clothes; 'Clay' is burley country folk, broad and genuine. Most jarringly, Vincent's skin is translucent white while Clay's a skin deep black. If the narrative depends upon their likeness, the camera *records* that they appear nothing alike.

In this abyss between speech and image, the naturalist codes of Hollywood cinema begin to slip out of phase with the viewer.[8] At first, we cannot believe our ears, then we begin to question our eyes. As these flip-flops accelerate, the film becomes a cinematic jabberwocky, a deliberate mixing of codes and cues, an experiment with the limits of sense and the

Sequence of camera and actor choreography circling from one profile to the other 360 degrees

capacity of our senses. In this regard, the film can be divided into three formal sequences, with transitions marked by the sound-image of an explosion. The first forms an audiovisual joke: a Johnny Cash song 'Ring of Fire' montaged with a violent car bomb. The second portion ends with the three gunshots when Vincent and Clay confront each other again in an eye-shaped bathroom. The third, and final, ends with the disembodied voice-over of Clay-Vincent's therapist and some snap-shots from Clay's new life. This last section, in which Clay militantly refuses the given regimes of signification lasts only minutes, as if formal conceit can no longer constrain the narrative. Each section effectively maps the dynamic shifts in codes of whiteness and its corresponding systems of measuring the black body. The schizo disjunction between speech and image propagated by extreme 'casting against type', at once rehearses and *intensifies* the problem of representing African-American experience through the warp and woof of whiteness.

RACISM AS HARMONIC ANALOGUE

The viewer's experience during the first section of the film, in which we are introduced to the characters, works (or rather, refuses to work) by scrambling the regime of representation and analogue resemblance. Similarly, the abstract machine of whiteness – racism as faciality – was historically actuated by a representational system of measured analogues, which it both projects and by which it is replicated. Indeed, the use of measure to re-constitute the body, maps the transformation of racist discourse from one concerning the other as alien or exotic to a regime which operates according to what Deleuze has elucidated as the "logic of

the same". [9]

A sampling along the epistemological lineage of 'scientific racism' exfoliates the White Face and reveals the pre-conscious lineaments of its cultural construction. [10] Camper's work marks the limit of an idealist regime of types. His most iconic measurement compared profiles of different races, abstracting the optimal slope from mouth to top of skull as the critical measure of beauty. Although a pseudo-Positivist measure, it addresses merely a neo-Platonic ideal rather than a material, statistical condition. The optimal ninety-degree slope was found solely in Greek sculpture, indicating both an aesthetic over-determination and the deficiency of this measure as a norm in the modern, empirical, sense. [11] Each race has its own proper range of deviation; there is an ideal angle for the African face as there is for the European, because each refers to a different aesthetic type. [12] Ugliness occurs only when the range for a racial type is exceeded. If the Greek prototype offers an aesthetic model appropriate for white Europeans, the African face exists in relation to this model, but is not fully circumscribed by its ordering. Whether regarded as a noble savage, beautiful in its own right, or primitive, there is an incommensurability of the black face with the European visage, an idea Kant argues in his *Critique of Judgement*. The ninety-degree plane of the perfect classical profile is perhaps the signifying wall upon which the White Face is drawn, yet its surface remains blank.

Only as this dualism wavers, as humanity is lowered from a divine position to occupy the same plane as nature (c.f. Darwin's natural selection or Mendel's heredity), could racism be reconfigured from disaggregated *similitude* to a mono-cultural inscription of *identifaction*. Indeed, the African physique would be re-territorialised by the white face rebus only when the norm and ideal shift directionality from the ideal as Platonic mimetic (a model, e.g. Greek statuary) for the production of copies (white) and debased simulacra (black) to a "regime of signs"[13] in which a statistical norm establishes the ideal. In the late-nineteenth century, Francis Galton could achieve what remained impossible for Laveter and Camper. By simultaneously establishing the autonomy of statistical and normative parameters for his eugenic project, Galton's work places all the 'races' upon the same bell-curve rather than in discrete categories. His photo composites, which superimpose several faces of a racial group (most infamously the Jewish population of London), do not establish an ideal type, but an ideal-average face. As Canguilhem and Bataille both argued, the normal had become the standard measure of monstrosity as deviance rather than the foreign. Racism operated now not according to a heterogeneous tableau of *human natures* (good, evil), but a smooth spectrum of *human behaviour* (healthy to sick).[14] The Other no longer refers to a different category, but only to degrees of differentiation, measured as a mimetic of standard deviation.

By flattening causality, the shift from souls to statistics eclipsed the *anciene régime* of racism by what Deleuze and Guattari more aptly named the *régime of faciality* (face-ism), which:

> operates by the determination of degrees of deviance in relation to the White-Man face, which endeavours to integrate nonconformist traits into increasingly eccentric and backwards waves… From the viewpoint of [this] racism there is no exterior, there are no people on the outside. There are only people who should look like us and whose crime it is not to be. The dividing line is not between inside and outside but rather is internal to the simultaneous signifying chains and successive subjective choices. Racism… propagates waves of sameness until all those who resist identification have been wiped out.[15]

Thus, as the statistico-probalistic topos attained prominence, the exotic black body as Other was *re-territorialised* as an *analogue*, as a frequency

exceeding the standard deviation along the all-encompassing spectrum of whiteness.

Ralph Ellison charts exactly this condition of whiteout. Indeed, the very first lines of *The Invisible Man* announce a world not so much gazed upon but constituted by the White Face:

> I am an invisible man. No, I am not a spook like those who haunted Edgar Allen Poe, nor am I one of your Hollywood movie ectoplasms. I am a man of substance, of flesh and bone, fiber and liquids – and I might even be said to possess a mind. I am invisible, understand, simply because people refuse to see me. Like the bodiless heads you see sometimes in circus sideshows, it is as though I have been surrounded by mirrors of hard distorting glass. When they approach me they see only my surroundings, themselves, or figments of their imagination – indeed, everything and anything except me.

In this prose of the white world,[16] the black body does not project, but neither does it receive the gaze of the white man. Nor is the black body an analogue of the white, either debased or heroic. It only *reflects* the face of whiteness, which projects a world of resemblance, or masks. In the shadowed crevices of white faciality, the African American takes his place as darker shade of pale.

In this 'logic of the same', fundamental equality is cemented upon the statistics of faciality, perhaps announcing the beginning of the end for the enlightenment-liberal topos. For the same reason, the assurance of preordained 'races' became insufficient for ideologies of purification, which became increasingly desperate and dangerous (c.f. the rapid expansion of Klu Klux Klan, the Third Reich's answer to the 'Jewish question'). Galton's eugenics, for example, promised not oppression and regimentation into fixed places, but an orthopaedics of whiteness through elimination of deviants, an attack upon the body as a symptom of faciality. Because it is as cruel as it is incompetent, the logic of the same engenders desperate acts - in the film as a car-bomb and in history as

149

lynching and gas-chamber. Galton's composites are one instance in the
actualisation of the white face as generic but total physiognomy.

white noise a type of sound characterised by a homogenous distribution of frequencies in a chaotic pattern, typically produced by an electrical or electronic apparatus.

But although we can recognise faciality as a distinctly modern mode of
racism incompatible with a naïve discourse of the Other, the measures
which finally install this regime of faciality remain elusive. Typical
explanations of colonial closure are incomplete, again because these tales
fail to engage its radical superficiality, *regarding* it only as an effect, and
searching for its meaning in remote depths. Instead, I would like to
experimentally suggest exploring a co-planar assemblage – the
organisation of noise. Perhaps it is through the organisation of sound that
the logo-centric White Face speaks. Is it this which the black cry of
outrage seeks to disrupt?

Indeed, when Ralph Ellison fleshed out the veil of whiteness Dubois
similarly had decried,[17] he invoked sound as a force capable of
convoluting the space the African-American occupies within the dominant
culture of American whiteness. Inspite of its title, the central trope of *The
Invisible Man* operates not according to visual motifs, nor via their
automatic privileging of space, but through a *sonic syncopation in time*:

> Invisibility, let me explain, gives one a slightly different sense of time,
> you're never quite on the beat. Sometimes you're ahead, sometimes you're
> behind. Instead of swift and imperceptible flowing of time, you are aware
> of its nodes, those points where time stands still or from which it leaps
> ahead. And you slip into the breaks and look around…

Neither 'outside' nor strictly marginal, the black man occupies the same space as the white man, indeed can only exist within its homogenous space. But for Ellison, the black body is *phase-shifted*, interleaved into an interstitial abjection by a syncopation, "never quite on the beat".

The beats to which the African-American cannot keep time but to which she is forced to march have been suggested by Jacques Attali's exegesis *Noise: The Political Economy of Music*. This text not only challenges the autonomy of musical discourse, but reverses the assumed flow of cultural materialisation (which traditionally treats sonic form as passive manifest-content, expressing an ideology originating elsewhere). For Attali, noise is not symptomatic, but predictive; its incorporeal forces precede and announce slower embodiments of cultural transformation (such as law or urbanism).

Attali delineates three modern European musical stages which he names representing, repetition, and composition.[18] In the first, harmonic represenation serves as the naturalisation for the ideological organisation of the colonial world.[19] If musicology defines harmony as a proportional progression of sound arranged on a diachronic, scale, this never constitutes simply a technique of composition. Instead, harmony "implies a system of measurement; in other words a system for the scientific, quantified representation of nature... the isomorphism of all representations."[20] Harmonics, Attali argues, creates an illusory, consensual image of order as a resemblance.[21] Musical representation expresses an analogue world of resemblance, with three effects. Firstly, harmonics fashion noise into an aesthetic measure, a pre-conscious criterion of judgement. Secondly, this representation configures the entire sensorium, thereby masking its revelation under the hegemony of the eye.[22] Lastly, the objects perceived though this system appear there as natural, therefore closing a hermeneutic loop.[23]

In these ways, harmonic representation was entwined with the normative, measured vision. This genealogy passes from the early interpreters of Vitruvius, through Kepler's cosmologies, Dürer's proportional system, to Wittkower's text on architectural order. Though diverse, all of these examples depend on a system of visual harmonics, using the diachronic scale as evidence of natural proportions. The iconoclastic naturalist D'Arcy Thomson even argued that, "the *harmony* of the world is made manifest by Form and Number... the poetry of Natural Philosophy [is embodied] in the concept of mathematical beauty" (emphasis added).[24] Thomson argues that classical proportional figures are, as one mathematician described the spiralling Golden Section, "the geometry of art and life" and these numbers are also found in diachronic scales. In this music of the spheres, harmonic ratio is naturalised and mystified at once, conflating the good and the beautiful such that measurements of racist pseudo-science are inseparable from this musical representation. For example, Mary Olmstead Stanton, a physiognomicist, writing in 1881, encapsulates these operations in her argument, "Form [is] a universal and determining principle... The form and shape of everything testifies to its character and rank among creations..." She then employs harmonic measures as the criteria for discerning tendencies of individuals and races.

Whether manifested as music, abstract measure or incarnated in the white-man's face, the juridical remit of harmony operates as an *analogue* system in which there is no outside, only a mimetic interiority. This system of representational analogues delimited the blank screen of whiteness, measuring its surface, regulating the proper disposition of its features and acceptable re-configurations. The black face stands not outside these representations, but formed a dissonant cord within this order of the beautiful.

MASKING HARMONIES

Masking tropes during Reconstruction suggest the difficulty of resisting analogue harmonic representation. The attempt to orthopaedically reconstruct the African-American into what Booker T. Washington called the 'New Black' sought to correct the cultural posture of the African

American through a physio-psychical therapy (the industrial agricultural education he founded at Tuskegee Institute). Another strain of this body-soul building topos sought a *representational orthopaedics*. As Henry Louis Gates has described:

> the features of African-Americans – mouth shape and lip size, the unique shape of the head... skin color, kinky hair – had been characterised and stereotyped so severely in popular American art, black intellectuals seemed to feel that nothing less than a full make-over or face-lift could cause... could begin to ameliorate the social conditions of the modern black American.[25]

John Henry Adams, for example, appropriated physiognomic rhetoric, attempting to re-code the features of the black man as beautiful and noble in his essay "Rough Sketches: a Study of the Features of the New Negro Man":

> Here is the new Negro man, tall erect, commanding, with a face as strong as Anglo Moses and yet every whit as pleasing and handsome as Ruben's favorite model. There is that penetrative eye... that broad forehead and firm chin... Such is the new Negro man, and he who finds the real man in the hope of deriving the benefits to be got by acquaintance and contact does not run upon him by chance, but must go over the paths of some kind of biography, until he gets a reasonable understanding of what it actually costs of human effort to be a man and at the same time a Negro.[26]

However, such attempts to correct white myopia by placing a mask of whiteness over the black subject can only affirm white faciality as totalising force. The assemblage of vision and sound via harmonic representation erected a mathematical landscape of possibility as the contours of white faciality, and in doing so forced this topology as a "consensual representation of the world".[27] Because of its analogue modality, one cannot reshuffle its signification without denying a place within the spectrum of humanity. Thus, after exhausting his optimism of reconstructing the white face by inclusion of the black identity with a rainbow spectrum of white light, Dubois left America, convinced the price of assimilation as analogue of whiteness – to be at the same time a man and a Negro – is death.

FROM ANALOGUE REPRESENTATION TO DIGITAL REPETITION

Thus, less than a hundred years after the civil war, the mask itself became a crucial site for racial identification and production of subjectivity. For Ralph Ellison invisibility is a kind of camouflage, a masking. But rather than mimic nature, it blends the black into white and at the same moment, white-outs this make-over:

> This mask, this wilful stylization and modification of the natural face and hands was imperative... the mask was the thing (and the 'thing' in more ways than) one and its function was to hide the humanity of Negroes thus reduced to sign and to repress the white audience's awareness of its moral identification with its own acts and to the human ambiguities pushed behind the mask.[28]

Yet it is through the operations of reconstruction and masking – with its techniques of recording, re-inscription and iterative repetition – that faciality as harmonic representation comes into crisis, or rather, reveals itself as a masking, a white noise. Indeed, the mask of whiteness reconstitutes the black body as an agent of arbitrary signification, but in doing so strains the 'natural' authority of its harmonic noise form.

The pervasive trope of the mask, such as deployed by Dubois and Ellison, is symptomatic of an acoustic shift towards a digital abstraction, announcing a different mode of faciality. Unlike the analogue harmonic representation – with its deviance from a normative model as racial degrees of separation – the digital recognises no model and no approximation but only the interchangeability of code and its arbitrary assignation. Such binary re-combination finds expression in what Attali calls *repetition*, in which 'natural' sensoria are dominated by technologies of mechanical reproduction:

The rupture of harmony seems to announce that the representation of society cannot induce real socialization, but leads to a more powerful, less signifying organization of nonsense. If this hypothesis holds true, then modernity is not the major rupture in the system for the chanellization of violence, the imaginary, and subversion... The probabalist transcendence of combinatrics by a code of dissonance [relies on] a code of cybernetic repetition, a society without signification. Music explores in this way the totality of sound matter... to the point of suicide of form.[29] For Attali, the shift from analogue measures to repetition merely provides a more efficient regime.[30] If harmony had abstracted the black skin as a debased version of whiteness, then repetition threatens even this identification by undermining all essential categories of meaning. The logic of the same, which always requires a model, shifted slightly into a logic of the serial which does not simulate a supposedly 'natural' reality or essential identification but replicates arbitrary, but for that reason powerfully, despotic dominations and assimilation.[31] There is no dissonance, but only re-combinations of a mask that is also the mould which constantly re-codes whiteness into slippery simulacra. Indeed, the move from harmonic representation (logic of the same) to digital repetition (logic of the serial) confirms the impossibility of challenging faciality through visual-spatial-corporeal tropes.[32] If analogue harmonic

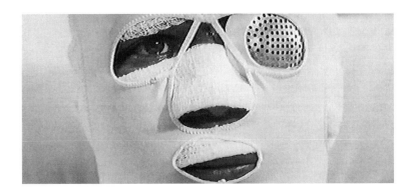

HIGHT

representation built a closed world, digital repetition is infinitely extensive and cannot be escaped without eroding the entire humanist project of equality – and exchangeability – upon which it knits its effacing mien.

white heat   1. a temperature higher than red heat, at which a body emits light

2. a state of intense excitation

Yet, if neither harmonic representation nor recorded repetition offer a *space* outside the White Face, perhaps it is possible, as Ellison seems to suggest, to appropriate an *intermezzo* in order to 'look around'. For Ellison writes himself out of the mask, not by finding a hole in space, but a gap in time. Similarly, Attali's third musical stage, which he calls *composition,* implies a potential for radical deterritorialisation of the White Face. Following Walter Benjamin, the techniques of art in the age of digital repetition has destabilising side-effects, draining the authority and aura that gird naturalist ordering: recording and the reproduction of speech reconstitutes the locus of power. Through its androids, it is author by itself that is speaking... and simulation, paradoxically, its caricatured double. For in drowning the discourse of established power, these androids simulate them...

> This simulation of the master's world leads to a questioning of the status of the master himself. Mechanisms for recording and reproduction on the one hand provide a technical body, a framework for representations, and on the other hand by presenting themselves as double, constitute a simulation of that power, destroy the legitimacy of representation...[33]

Engendered by the machinery of communication and reproduction, and inseparable from these techniques, this composition entails a *cybernetic* ontology. The technical body of repetition does not record resemblance to a model, nor simply differences and deviancies, but the constructed, depositic conditions of normative representation and its repetition. This music thus produces hybrid simulations, 'androids', that eventually reveal themselves as simulacra, copies without originals, free signifiers of recombination and multiplication. The early experiments of rap, a cybernetic music *par excellence*, suggest just such an immediate, urban politics of sound. The literal devices of recording – turntables, microphones, sampling, and playing (scratching) records themselves – became the instruments for composition.[34] It is therefore interesting to note, as Ron Eglash has argued, that fractal sound analyses reveal rap music is composed according to a completely different paradigm from harmonic systems, modernist 'serial' music and even jazz or pop. All of the latter retain a fractal proportioning rule. Rap, on the other hand, disrupts "analogue representation by digital coding" offering "possibilities for cybernetic innovation" and hybridisation away from essentialist identification.[35]

This mode of composition also seems related to the militant resistance Cornel West has described as 'witnessing', defined as techniques of recording remaking, and reinvention.[36] This witnessing, however, does not initially manifest visually but as an acoustic text. As West argues, "the 'urtext' of black culture is neither word nor book, not an architectural monument or a legal brief. Instead, it is a 'guttural cry and a wrenching moan'."[37] The logo-centrism implied by the insistence on the authoritative voice as the 'ur-text' seems displaced by its role as a exo-literate documentation: the slave song, the spiritual, the scream, is a tool of recording and repeating an event, an almost sacrificial expression of agony and ecstasy as noise-matter.

The uncanny stop, this syncopated stutter, ruptures the stoic countenance of faciality, rendering the white face visible. Most importantly these examples suggest a different understanding of sound as matter – an envelope of potentials and qualities that can not be understood at a distance, but only traversed. The lived condition of noise and its media of modulation and conduction entail performative rather than definitive operations. It is characterised not by notes, entablatures, time signatures, or any other hylomorphic codings, but through experimental immersions and infinite re-codings: feedback loops, pulsings, resonances, and intensifications. In contrast, the representational order is hylomorphic in the extreme, treating all matter as formless and inert, requiring that form be imposed from the outside in order to make objects of knowledge and sense. Composition suggests an *epigenesis* – a continual becoming upon a topological landscape of improbability – where the surfaces are not frozen faces, fixed signifiers, or coded expressions but an improvisory landscape of virtual potentiality. To regain vision, to shake off the encumbering mask, is to *compose* a line of flight in noise. How does one compose such a soundtrack of escape? How does one ride this sonic boom?

SUPERFICIAL CYBORG SPIRITUALS

Suture elaborates a song of cybernetic emancipation, as even its title foregrounds tropes of reconstruction and assemblage. As previously suggested, in the first section the disjunction between narrative speech and form is merely dissonant, effectively describing a domain of harmonic representation.

The second section introduces the second of Attali's noise epochs, repetition, by documenting the laborious reconstruction of Clay's face into Vincent's. As doctors and x-rays describe the rupture and reshaping of Clay's body, the camera develops a careful measured comparison of his shattered face and Vincent's. In fact, Clay appears on screen exactly as he did before the plastic surgeries, which can thus be understood primarily as a masking of Clay under the signifying order of whiteness.[38] Moreover, an exegesis of physiognomics is deployed throughout this section, which frequently juxtaposes Vincent's and Clay's faces in profile, uncannily echoing Camper's work. Indeed, as if replicating the favoured techniques of physiognomy, all the characters are predominately filmed in either profile or facing straight into the camera. The camera serves as a clinical apparatus; like a rotating x-ray machine, a shot will begin with a profile of two characters facing each other, and then slowly revolve around the figures until it stops in a profile on the other side.[39]

These tensions come to a literal head in the image of Clay's shattered face. In this regard, the audio-visual montage constantly affiliates Clay with the electronic hums of the telephones, medical equipment, and industrial machinery.[40] His doctors employ video and photographic images of Vincent as models for the plastic-surgery. His face is seen through a white mask of gauze bandages. The psychic identity of Clay is similarly reconstructed. Clay learns of his supposed past via mechanically reproduced images, photographs and video recordings. His psychoanalyst provides a pedagogy of molar identity, instructing Clay to decipher the codes of his dream-images as signs of repressed content. Through such psychoanalytic clichés, the morselated identity Clay is reintegrated as the mirror-image identity of 'Vincent'. Yet, Clay does not 'see himself seeing himself', when he looks in the mirror, nor does he see Vincent. Instead, the *viewer* confronts the cold white eyes of the White Face, staring not at him, but through his body.

At the same time, however, Clay has become a recording device, his body literally stitched and inscribed with the atrocities of whiteness. Transposing the tradition of the North-African mystic who forms and breathes life into clay, the film reconstitutes 'Clay' as a golem, vitalised by the technologies of replication and recording. This android simulacrum, Clay-Vincent is a hybrid subject, a cyborg, whose 'technical body' is both produced by the regimes of White signification and recording, but which threaten its authority by prodigious recoding and dissimulative effects.[41] Just as Ellison undermined a naturalist hegemony via 'invisibility', the artificiality of the film's mise-en-scene undermines the binarisms – form/content, black/white, machine/organism, animal/human, nature/culture – which underlie both harmonic and repetitive faciality.

159

Technologies of (re)production
recording and reforming

The film's third section charts the limits of white *faciality* with a compositional mode. The Clay-Vincent cyborg waits in the shower, shotgun in unsteady hands. Seen in an overhead shot, the specially designed set resolves into a dissected eye. Clay and Vincent are on either side of the translucent white shower curtain, which resembles a glaucoma-clouded lens, the white mask. The curtain is drawn back. The brothers are face to face. The screen goes black. Our vision fails. Three noises, three gun shots, three shattered silences. The trauma of seeing what used to be Vincent's face, now literally erased into a glistening black wound, floods Clay's memory, which now returns in force. While the analyst wants to stabilise Clay's identity through emphasising his unity, the Clay-Vincent cyborg no longer sees the world through a white mask but sees the mask itself, and begins to question the status of his masters. If Ellison's invisible man turns towards his condition to dissect his status, Clay-Vincent reterritorialises the absurdity of his condition. He no longer attempts to represent a reality imposed from elsewhere, nor attempts to repeat a code of truth. Clay has not become formless, but open to multiplicity and literal poly-vocality.

His psychoanalyst is horrified when Clay decides to continue living as Vincent. As the film fades to black through several snap-shots from Clay's future life, the analyst's closing voice-over declares that, while Clay-Vincent may drive Vincent's expensive cars, go to the exclusive clubs, and have all the trappings of Vincent's life, his new life is not real, only a simulation, for it constitutes a false identity. Throughout the film, the analyst's voice has provided an authoritative framing narrative, one which introduces the story ("What you are about to see… ") as clinically told

Clay re-forms his subjectivity

from a third party's objective point of view. Of course, this role is immediately complicated as it is drained, the only tension hinges upon whether an explanation for this extreme indulgence shall be offered. To its credit, the film offers none.

Thus, the irresolution of the entire film finds its humorous nadir in the refrain of its theme song, *Ring of Fire* – a version written by Johnny-The Man in Black-Cash, sung by the Welsh Tom Jones, mimicking James-Godfather of Soul-Brown. The analyst's over-determining voice is disrupted by its sharp juxtaposition with this effervescent tune. The viewer's response – usually a momentary silence followed by laughter – is on the one hand an ironic snigger, but also the laughter induced by shock. Such a reflex response negotiates the attack on the codes of sensibility as simultaneous a *jouissance* and trauma. In this case, a trauma in that the film has literally shattered its representational surface in front of us and left us with nothing; ecstasy in energy unleashed by this cataclysmic breakdown in the abstract machine of faciality. Our laughter therefore produces a ripple, a discontinuity across the surface upon which 'whiteness' comes to signify itself, to measure its domain, to subject all to its aesthetic sensibility.

When Ellison invoked sound to disrupt the white veil of naturalism, or when the technology of the music industry was appropriated in hip-hop, or a film refuses to resolve image and narrative into a reflexive closed logic, the stony face of whiteness become slippery – but only momentarily. The film, for example, is a one-off, a novelty that works, if it can be said to work at all, by a clever wilfulness. Our laughs decrease each time this pratt-fall of the White Face, covered in cream pie, is rehearsed.

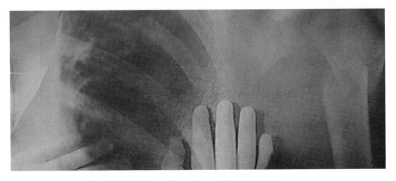

Reading the depth of the body on the surface with a haptic vision

The performance is never as funny the second time around; the shock is mitigated by expectation. The digital white face slowly incorporates this rupture as a pock-mark, or even as a distinguishing feature, a feather in its liberal humanist cap, evidence of its multi-cultural street cred. Ultimately, therefore, it is not a question of for whom we speak (or whom we represent), but in what timbre our enunciations are put forth, how we continually re-inscribe and transmit their carrier signal. What is the resonant frequency that shatters the stony face of whiteness?

NOTES

1 Isaac Hayes. Theme from *Shaft*. Stax Records, 1974.

2 *I'm Going to Get You Sucka!* Dir. Keenen Ivory-Wayanes, MGM, 1988.

3 Gilles Deleuze and Felix Guattari, *A Thousand Plateaus: Capitalism And Schizophrenia,* University of Minnesota Press, Minneapolis,1987, p. 168.

4 Deleuze and Guattari, pp. 170-171.

5 Deleuze and Guattari, p. 176.

6 Oxford English Dictionary. The other section heading (i.e., white noise, white heat) are also derived from the OED.

7 *Suture*. Written, produced and directed by Scott McGehee and David Siegel, Samuel Goldwyn, 1992. The film's reception by the popular critical press demonstrated its lack of imagination. The famous critic Roger Ebert offered this facile comment on the films strong formalism: "The co-directors... have a design school background, and are apparently more concerned with how the movie looks than how it plays. That is an approach that sometimes yields benefits... to evoke an aura of mystery, the notion that something is happening beneath the surface. *Suture* seems to be all surface." (*Chicago Sun Times,* 7 August 1994). Could not the trope of depth be itself a superficial effect of the radical surface of whiteness?

8 Although the film's narrative mirrors Hitchcock's *Spellbound,* the scrambling of naturalistic codes leads to a profound sense of vertigo. This is exactly the effect Ellison described as his goal in the framing portions of *The Invisible Man* – an attempt to chart an espace from the dominating planes of realism and fantasy, which has been called a strategy of the grotesque. Refer to, Fritz Gysin, "The Grotesque in American Negro Fiction", *The Cooper Monographs,* Basel, 22, 1975, p. 189.

9 Deleuze's term, the logic of the same, is an ordering of concepts perpetuated by faciality, and for Deleuze is implicated in the fashioning of 'molar', or collective identifications of fascist essentiality.

10 For a clear and devastating critique of the relationship between race and science, including recent iterations, refer to Stephen J. Gould, *The Mismeasure of Man,* Penguin

Books, London,1997, second edition.

11 For a discussion of Camper, Lavater and other similar scientific studies as form of corporeal connoisseurship refer to: Barbara Stafford, *Body Criticism: Imaging the Unseen in Enlightenment Art and Medicine,* MIT Press, Cambridge, Mass.,1993, pp. 84-103.

12 Kant's aesthetic judgement also delineates different aesthetic types for each race and aesthetic judgements internal to each (i.e., the beautiful reveals itself differently in and for the European and the African). In short, races define limits of aesthetic commensurablility. This argument occurs in one of the most neglected but precarious sections from *The Critique of Judgement*, which I have explored elsewhere.

13 Deleuze and Guattari , pp. 140-141.

14 For a discussion of Galton's work, and his role in establishing the autonomy of statistical law, refer to: Ian Hacking, *The Taming of Chance,* Cambridge University Press, Cambridge, 1990, chapter 21.

15 Deleuze and Guattari, pp. 178.

16 A play on Foucault's use of *Don Quixote* in a chapter of *Les Mots et les Choses.*

17 F.W. Dubois described the condition of the African-American as the use of the white measure, "a peculiar sensation, the double-conscience, this sense of always looking at one's self through the eyes of others, of measuring one's soul by the tape of a world that looks in amused contempt and pity". As quoted in: Henry Louis Gates Jr. and Cornel West, *The Future of the Race,* Alfred A Knoff, New York, 1996, p. 87.

18 Attali's prior stage of music, sacrificing, notably operates via similitude and indexical relation-ships to social organisations.

19 Jacques Attali, *Noise: The Political Economy of Music*, Manchester University Press, Manchester, 1985, p. 3.

20 Attali, p. 60.

21 Attali, pp. 59–60.

22 Attali challenges an understanding of form as supplementary to content or as its expression. Consequently, he problematises music's appearance as if it is content-less, or rather, autonomous.

23 Attali, pp. 20-21.

24 D'Arcy Thompson, *On Growth and Form*, Cambridge University Press, Cambridge, 1961, abridged edition.

25 Henry Louis Gates Jr., 'The Face and Voice of Blackness' preface to *Facing History: The Black Image in American Art 1710 to 1940,* by Guy C. McElroy, Bedford Arts, San Francisco, 1990, p. xxxix.

26 John Henry Adams, "Rough Sketches for the New Negro Man", as quoted in Gates (1990), p. xxxix.

27 Attali, p. 59.

28 Ralph Ellison, as quoted in Gates (1990), p. xxix.

29 Attali, p. 83.

30 Walter Benjamin's *Work of Art in the Age of Mechanical Reproduction* is clearly instrumental to Attali's argument, which draws out the ramifications of that essay's last section on the relationship between aesthetics and politics.

31 Attali situates the shift to repetition in the mid-nineteenth century, but does not consider this an epistemic rupture in the relationship of music to culture. Instead this historical break concerned the dissolution of the classical mathesis into a bureaucratisation of noise.

32 The abstract machine of faciality produces the body, around which all the metaphors of space and vision turn: "The decoding of the body implies an overcoding of the face; the collapse of corporeal coordinates or milieus implies the construction of a landscape. The codes create the face, and it is through the face of whiteness that they exert their power" (Deleuze and Guattari, p. 181). Hence the limitations of phenomenological or hermeneutic models of knowledge.

33 Attali, p. 86-87.

34 This is not to say that they cannot be re-territorialised, as hip-hop has been by the recording industry. We are speaking not of transcending faciality, but of a constant and militant refusal and affirmation of other possibilities.

35 Ron Eglash, "African Influences in Cybernetics", in *The Cyborg Handbook,* ed. Chris Hables Gray, Routledge, New York, 1995.

36 Cornel West and Henry Louis Gates Jr. (1996), p. 93.

37 Cornel West and Henry Louis Gates Jr. (1996), p. 84.

38 In fact, the film presents a formal catalogue of stereotypes deployed by Hollywood cinema. For example,

on his birthday, an opera singer serenades Clay. In a cheap plastic top hat, he is the reincarnation of Sambo.

39 Recalling Hitchock's revolving camera, a filmic device which disrupts naturalist representation by foregrounding the camera's movement, these exacting shots construct a cacophony of signifiers that no longer have a relationship, let alone a determining causation, to meaning.

40 The only other noises Clay is associated with lead either to ironic destruction or forms a cruel but effective joke, as when he is listening to opera (see above).

41 Clay's reconstitution as a cyborg clearly follows Donna Haraway's conditions for becoming a cybernetic subject. She established three binary machines of representation, each of which must be ruptured for the constitution of a cyborg subjectivity. These are the nature/culture, human/animal, and physical/immaterial. Donna Haraway, *Simians, Cyborgs, and Women: The Reinvention of Nature*, Free Association Books, London,

1991. I remain less convinced of the liberating potential of the cyborg persona or the tropes of fragmentation Haraway employs. Notably, Hollywood has eschewed black cyborgs, content instead the Teutonic hard body of Arnold Schwarzenegger's *Terminator* or Rutger Hauer's replicant in *Blade Runner*.

42 Similarly, Deleuze and Guattari's critique of traditional psychoanalysis explicitly attacks it as exposing the regimes of oedipal faciality but of keeping these regimes intact. They argue for a radical deterritorialisation they call 'shizo-analysis'. Similarly, what is at stake in the film is an attempt to explode the edifice of content-form. While its conceit is a valorous and energising attempt its audacity remains perhaps too visible, to obvious.

IMAGE CREDITS

All images are from the film: *Suture*. Written, produced and directed by Scott McGehee and David Siegel, Samuel Goldwyn, 1992. Permission requested.

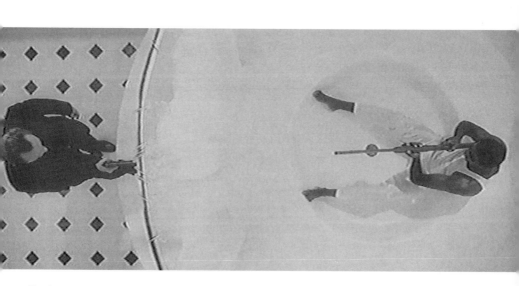

The shower scene: eye, gun and the violence of vision

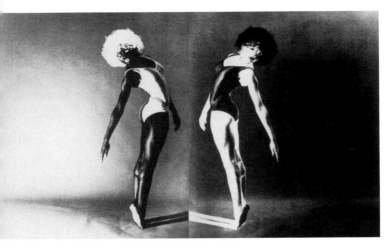

John Hilliard, *Dawn*, 1984

WHITE LIGHT AND ITS OTHER
PHOTOGRAPHS OF JOHN HILLIARD

MICHAEL UWEMEDIMO

DIVINE LIGHT AND THE VEIL OF SHADOWS

Philo of Alexandria, in his exegesis of the vatic, describes the prophet as one who has "within him a noetic sun [from which] shadowless beams of light give him clear apprehension of things invisible to the sense".[1] This shadowless light, which Philo does not conceive of as metaphoric, casts its clear beam through the neo-Platonic tradition. It is a light which emanates from Platonism, broadly constructed, and whose angles of incidence inform many theories of illumination, both epistemological and

metaphysical, in thinkers as radically different as Augustine and Descartes.
This light, however, cannot but throw shadows. Its shadow, bleached from
the supernatural, is displaced to the realm of the natural, *is,* indeed,
nature; and it is in nature, that vale of shadows, that light is always
shadowed. Despite Philo's banishment of shadows to the mundane, light
and its dark other are, of course, a frequent cosmic couple. One need
think only of Zoraster, Mani, or Augustine. Light's haunting double is
darkness.

Light, natural and supernatural, is 'white' by default; in Goethe's telling
phrase "white is the representative of light".[2] For Newton 'white' light is
the light of the everyday, a proposition he proceeds to prove with less
than persuasive argument. Briefly, his line is this. If red light is that in
which white paper appears red, green light is that in which white paper
appears green, then white light must be that in which white paper appears
white.[3] That his conclusion is often taken to be transparently evident only
points to the problematic and paradoxical opacity of 'white' light. What
would it mean for light to be white, that which we see and see through?
When asked to imagine a transparent whiteness, we are forced, as was
Wittgenstein, to admit that we simply do not know what it is that we are
supposed to imagine, we draw a blank.[4] Furthermore, that very blankness
is by default also white, as Newton's litmus test for light illustrates. The
relationship between whiteness, light, blankness, and the telling surfaces
of inscription – paper and skin particularly – is intriguingly complex. A
printer's blank, for which a 'White' is a synonym, is by definition and
default white; Jefferson infamously asserted that white skin is the surface
which makes legible the blushing signs of shame and tenderness; and as
Richard Dyer has observed, photographic paper is the white ground
which conspires with the transparency of that privileged glowing and
blushing white subject.[5] Crossing the road in dense white fog would
perhaps render the opacity of 'white' light clear as day. It is not my aim
here to try to locate accurately the puzzle of a transparent white either in
metaphysical necessity, physical process, or logical grammar. This puzzle

may be left here simply as a puzzle. Indeed, the very hazy indeterminacy of the term and conceptions of 'white' light, and consequently its shadow-crowded polyvalence, is one of o⌐ central concerns.

If the whiteness of natural light is somewhat problematic, supernatural light, with the reach of grace, draws a bright veil over such conceptual conundrums, and, so veiled, shines whiter than white. The experience, described in *A Sense of Presence*, in which God "appeared as a soft slightly blurred white light" is not an untypical phenomenological account of divine apprehension.[6] There are many such in a range of literatures from the prophetic to the psychoanalytic. The new testament offers a host of similar examples, in Matthew, for instance, Jesus appears "his raiment white as the light"(17:2), or elsewhere "white as snow"(28:2). *The Near-Death-Experience* catalogues numerous reports of the whiteness of the 'being of light' which apparently awaits us at the end of a dark tunnel.[7] This positive whiteness could be adduced also *via negativa*, through darkness and black light. *Luca Mikrokosma (The Ray of Microcosm)* is an epic of South Slav non-academic vernacular philosophy by the Bishop-Prince of Montenegro.[8] It elaborates a dualistic metaphysics and cosmogony which, though somewhat unorthodox, shares with numerous metaphysical systems and cosmogonies many structural features and qualitative attributes grounded in the binary configuration of light/white/dark/black. Located between the bordering worlds of Light and of Darkness is the earth. The sky of Hades, the world of darkness, is negatively illuminated, or perhaps drained of light, by its own black sun. Whiteness, it seems, has a determinate opposite in a way that no other colour has, apart of course from black; it is bi-polar. Harder to imagine perhaps is that 'dazzling darkness' which Pseudo-Dionysus describes at the nadir/apogee of 'apophatic' ascent to the 'superessential' divinity.[9] This black brilliance finds its own polar partner in that white blinding light that fell upon Saul on the road to Damascus. Between a dazzling darkness and a blinding whiteness there is an indeterminate difference that borders uncertainly on identity.

These instances of 'white' light and its other bear tellingly on the central focus of this paper. That dark globe of Hades may be imagined as being not dissimilar to an image of the sun on a photographic negative. Perhaps the way in which many might conceive of a dazzling darkness or blinding white is by analogy to a technology that has long offered itself as a model for many human faculties. As Lee Bailey argues in *The Skull's Darkroom: The Camera Obscura and Subjectivity*, this proto-photographic apparatus figures, in thinkers from Leonardo to Locke, as a root metaphor for, and model of, subjectivity, mind, soul, various psychological theories of projection, and of course vision; its technological avatars continue to inform such models.[10] The dazzling blackness of much negative theology can be pictured as the stain, the positive index of light on a negative; Saul's blinding whiteness as the bleaching over-exposure of light in the positive print which negates, veils with light, the image. If, as Wittgenstein

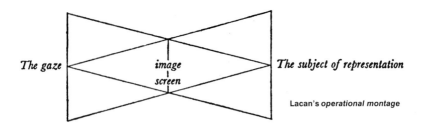

The gaze   *image*   *The subject of representation*
             screen

Lacan's *operational montage*

argued, white is the lightest colour, then light, in black and white photography and negative theology at least, is both white and black.[11]

BLACK LIGHT, WHITE SHADOWS — TORCH AND CAMERA

I See a Black Light (1987) [refer to colour plate 6], the title of a photographic work by John Hilliard, calling to mind as it does the 'dark rays of light' of negative theology, serves as an apposite transitional trope. Both are concerned, each in the different registers of the mystical and the semiotic, with white light and darkness as signs of presence/absence. *I*

See a Black Light plays on and with this uncertain play of light in the photographic process, as do many of the photographic works of John Hilliard. It is these works, rather than any superlunary speculations about the metaphysics of black and white light, that informs for the most part the body of this paper. We shall see how the whiteness of light in these photographs, which always threatens to spill into its dark other, is set to work in a series of differences and binary oppositions which sets up rather rigorous semantic structures which are nonetheless richly polysemous. This piece, ink on a large canvas, bears the printed double image of a figure in a body-stocking holding a torch, the figure mirrors itself in negative. Each image appears to conflate the positive and the negative, and confounds the immediate identification of either as such. The black figure we associate in black and white photography with a negative image. Some of the reasons for, and implications of, this assumption will be touched upon in what follows. The beam of the torch, however, betrays it as the positive, whose rays dissolve into the black light that spills from the torch of the spectral white figure, the negative.

The scene is "spare and reduced", composed of a minimum of elements.[12] As the artist has commented, the employment of black and white photography figures in this strategy of "draining, reducing and veiling".[13] Black and white are the first colour terms to be encoded in language; if a language has only two colour terms, such as Papuan Dani, they will be these.[14] This is as might be expected, Hardin and Maffi observe, "lightness and darkness are of course the most salient visual experiences, and so we would anticipate that they would be encoded first".[15] This doubtless goes some way to account for their role as primordial elements in many cosmogonies, as well as their capacity to so reduce the visual field that the structures of that field are rendered visible. It would not take a great degree of further reductive abstraction to arrive from the elements of this image at Lacan's famous diagram of the subject and gaze, the resonance and salience of which will become clear.[16]

Within this reduced field the intensity with which we seek out significant detail is increased. Searching the picture' the beam of the torch lights on, and lights up, our demanding gaze. As the beam is mirrored in negation within the image, so it mirrors the gaze of the photographer and spectator alike, throws such a light on them as to force them to throw their own shadows across the image, just as the figure throws its own bright shadow. "In the scopic field" Lacan proposed in one of his lectures on the gaze, "everything is articulated in an antinomic way – on the side of things, there is the gaze, that is to say, things look at me, and yet I see them".[17] The spectator negates herself to become all eye, pure vision, but the image returns the gaze and with it the body of the spectator – as an image of the other. And, in becoming aware of her own presence in front of the image, is made aware of the absence of the photographer. The shadows the photographer and spectator throw are negatives of one another, in the way that each figure in the image is the shadow of the other. The camera too is forced to mark its absence. The torch itself, as productive instrument of light, can be read as a mirroring of the camera, which as the receptive instrument of light, stands as the negative to the torch's positive. The torch, as the mark of the absent camera, is positioned so as to appear as a phallic apparatus, and its beam so as to suggest the role of light as phallic agent of positive presence and the privilege of the visible. It is, if you like, a seminal light, a light that produces its objects within the horizon of its transcendental limit. Yet that very positivity is literally negated, and light burns the mark of its own absence. While the beam of light points towards the fact that light is a necessary condition of vision, its dissolution into its own negative reminds one of photography's power to render certain things invisible.

The black body-stocking, a second-skin which masks the first, both renders the sex of the figure indeterminate and makes the figure a shadow of itself. The first skin, white, is a negative of the black second skin, which is again negated into whiteness. Opposites pass into each other. The photograph itself, in its materiality and indexicality, performs these same functions of masking, shadowing, and mirroring. It doubles the dynamic of the doubled image it bears.

THE DOPPELGANGER

The *doppelganger*, Andrew Webber claims:

> can be said to subvert the aesthetic principle of figuration precisely by a virtuoso act of imitation – duplicating the 'real' by the unreal. The subjective spook at once threatens and underpins the objective claims of realism; it has something of the effect of a photographic negative. [18]

Black Light, then, figures the double both within the photograph, and the photograph as the double. The photograph stands as double in relation to its objects of representation through an analogous relation of negation as the positive print does to the negative. As Metz observed, the scopic specificity of photography is marked by the empirical fact of the absence of its objects of representation. [19] The logic of the double in this photograph, structured by the quasi-logical, yet contradictory potentialities, of light/white/dark/black, places the 'real' and the realism of the medium in critical tension. The lure of the image draws the gaze towards a scene that mirrors its own procedure. The photograph – duplication and negation of the real – is composed of a duplicate in negative. The positive image appears as an absence, or negative, which is supplemented by its double, or shadow, which in turn, following a Derridian logic of supplementarity, appears as the positive and threatens to eclipse the 'real'. This lack within the subject and object of representation points to a lack in the 'real self' (it is dressed as shadow, as a cloak of insubstantiality) and by extension to the 'real' itself. This lack in the 'real' is itself supplemented by the medium of realism *par excellence*, that which offers itself as a transparent window on to the real. Yet the transparency of the medium is shadowed and rendered opaque by the doubling and shadowing. This series of moves, which allows one order to slip into the next and back through its opposition in a kind of mobeus loop, is effected in part by the use of black and white – just as a 'dazzling darkness' slips into the blinding light, or as the negative makes the positive print. The unstable symmetry of black and white, itself an asymmetrical property of these colours, allows one to be the other, while remaining absolutely different. Borges wrote a short story about a man who kept clasped in his palm a one sided disk, an object impossible to imagine as a glass of transparent milk; the impossible geometry of this disk suggests the equally impossible symmetry that allows the absolute difference and identity of black and white, they are two sides of the same (ones-sided) coin.[20]

The *doppelganger* too is a figure of both absolute identity and absolute difference. This image condenses all the properties of that figure – shadow, mirror image, double, vision of immortality and harbinger of death. These various aspects are all classic characteristics of the *doppelganger* motif, as Webber has argued in his discussion of the double in German literature,[21] and it is Otto Rank who famously claimed that the myth of the doppelganger is itself inversely doubled – it is the light of immortality and the shadow of death.[22]

Indeed, we encounter both these dimensions in the work. The headpiece of the black stocking in negative becomes a deaths head, a skull, bone white. It stands as the shadow of death. The shadow, however, is white, and luminosity in photography is a sign of presence – for it signals reflectance and thus substance. Thus, moving through the same operational logic outlined above, the white shadow, the double, is more fully present than the 'real'. It is a lethal usurper. Yet we do not merely find here an allegorical or emblematic figuration of a motif, arbitrarily chosen by the author. As already noted, photography itself is figured, and it is the photographic mode of representation that determines the appositeness of this motif. If cinema, as Godard asserted with pointed irony, is death twenty-four times a second, then photography is a still death. Yet the memorial photograph – either taken after death and held as living memory against it or an image stolen from life and denied to death – indicates the intensity with which we look into the photograph for signs of life. In this sense the photographic double offers the promise of immortality, just as the luminous shadow might suggest not only death but the immortal soul.

MAKE-UP, MASKS, AND STAINED CLOTH

Where as *Black Light* is organised around a literal doubling of image, *Impression of Death* (1987) is organised thematically around a double motif – art and life, or, if that seems too nineteenth-century a formulation, representation and the real. Again black and white are central to this

organisation. Here we face an actor, over his shoulder, as he removes his make-up, the impression of which is stained into a black towel which he holds, in a dressing room mirror. That the figure is an actor, rhetorically signals a concern for the staging of representation. The mirror through which we see his partially painted face suggests at once the frame of the proscenium arch, and thus theatre as 'mirror of life', and

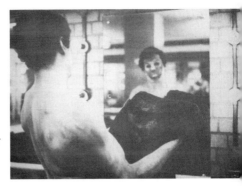

John Hilliard, *Impression of Death*, 1987

the picture frame, the 'window onto the world'. Importantly, the face which we see mirrored is partly masked by a film of black or white grease paint, as the real absence of that face is masked by film itself. I say black *or* white paint advisedly – the white stain on the towel suggests white paint, however, the face, which belongs to what appears to be a white body, is marked by black. The transparent window of the photograph, then, appears as far from clear and opens not onto 'life' but elaborate and ambiguous artifice. The black/white opposition between skin and second skin, as it did with the body stocking in *Black Light*, sets up an oppositional ambivalence. Not a static binary, black or white, but a zone of productive indeterminacy, a grey zone. Representation does not stand

John Hilliard, *Dark Shadow*, 1984

simply opposed to the 'real' but is one of its moments, art is an aspect of life.

The motifs of face, mask, and mirror as representational surface are echoed and condensed by the richly allusive image of the face stained into the towel. These works themselves are produced by spraying ink directly onto the fabric of the canvas. Here the association of death shroud and photograph is forceful. The Turin shroud, that most famous of death shrouds, has of course, though perhaps somewhat doubtfully, been evidenced as an example of proto-photography.[23] Such an association involves, not only the dialectic of death and representation, such as fascinated Bataille after Hegel[24] – this photograph, as has *Black Light*, has been collected in a catalogue aptly titled *Vanitas*[25] – but also the photograph as fetish. Interestingly enough, it seems likely that the dark negative image of the shroud precipitated the shift in representations of Jesus, which occurred not long after it was displayed as the most sacred of relics, from the dark, short, curly-haired, and often unbearded figure of much early Byzantine art, to the fair, tall figure that we are so familiar with today – the dark negative as a model for the white Christ.[26]

From shroud we move to veil. *Dark Shadow* (1984), is composed of two identical portraits of a veiled woman. Identical, that is, save that one is the negative image. This woman is both bride and widow, and thus this piece is also driven by the symbolic dynamics of black and white. Of most interest for my purposes here, however, are the black and white veils themselves. Both of the first two works which have been discussed deploy strategies of shadowing and masking, structurally and thematically, in such a way that these elements "all in turn collude in a rebuttal of the aspiring transparency of photography".[27] Here is Lacan: "In what is presented to me as a space of light, that which is gaze is always a play of light and opacity".[28] While the picture plane is often spoken of as a transparent window, Alberti suggests it is best conceived of as a veil across the visual field.[29] That veil is introduced here as itself a pictorial element.

The next work I want to look at, *Dawn* (1984), leads initially away from veiling and masking, and back into shadows. Its relation to *Masquerade* (1982) [refer to colour plate 7], a piece which can be read as a complication of *Dawn*'s strategies, will bring the argument back to the picture plane as veil, mask, screen, and, eventually, as grid. Whereas it is the beam of light that betrays the positivity and negativity of the images in *Black Light*, in *Dawn* it is the shadows. I have contended that the white/light figure in black and white photography is privileged as the positive image, as its reflectance is taken to signal its presence. As Dyer has argued, the ballerina is the very image of the luminous white woman.[30] And certainly, it is uncommon to see a black person with white hair, unless albino – those who are all the more 'black' for their 'whiteness'. All these factors conspire to confound and unsettle the expectations of the viewer before this image. The title itself is in ironic complicity with the strategy. As a result, the process of racial designation, which depends on particular conceptions of whiteness and blackness and where they are likely to be located, is stalled. We are forced to look at skin tone without being able to subsume it to specific racial categories. Instead we catch ourselves searching for clues, we find ourselves needing to know.

These dynamics are productively complicated in *Masquerade*. Again, black and white organise the visual and semantic structure of this image. Movement and stasis, of both the camera and its objects, also work to order the visual field. Here both race and gender are figured in a way which seems less governed by the demands of a particular photographic effect. The now formulaic pairing of white mask and black skin is subtly undone. The white mask of masculinity, itself rigid and immobile, is set in motion to reveal the black face of a woman. The face, however, the privileged sign of authentic presence, is itself made up. The make-up masks what in fact appears to be the face of a white male. There is no simple unmasking here, no sudden rending of the veil, no immediate access to the real. The immanent critique to which John Hilliard opens photographic discourse is not of the naïve model of ideology critique, which would simply draw open the curtain of false consciousness, exposing superstition with science. Rather, these works make reflexively visible the medium and its mediation. "The foregrounding of mediation" Michael Newman observed of this image, "opens up a split between the image as it is read and the image as   The mask, the painted face, the screen and the grid are all present as pictorial elements in *Façade* (1982) [refer to colour plate 8]. The title is compositionally present in this piece as it is in *Masquerade*. Thus it gains an emblematic character which perhaps justifies the searching out of clues which serve an allegorical elaboration. Such an elaboration of this image would be comparable in many ways to that of *Masquerade*. There is no room here, however, to explore it in its singularity. I have reproduced it because of the way in which it pictorially condenses, in the screen behind the figure, the veil and the grid – that is, Alberti's picture plane and that of Dürer. Such a condensation serves to lead us to another work via the motif of the grid. It is a work in a somewhat different register, yet which nevertheless gives an insight into the dynamics we have been exploring at an early moment of their inception. It is the grid which forms the compositional framework of *Camera Recording its own Condition* (1971).

Camera Recording its own Condition marks the beginnings of a body of work which "addresses itself to photographic representation through an acknowledgement of the ambiguities and constraints peculiar to the medium"[33]. John Roberts claims "The work from this period (1970-73) is perhaps the only photo-based conceptual art which is actually discursively engaged with the mechanics and chemistry of the photographic document".[34] Produced in the ferment of Conceptualism and against the backdrop of Minimalism we see traces of both. The extremes of the grid, which calls to mind the grids of Sol Lewitt, tend towards the monochromes, at one end of the achromatic scale, of Ad Reinhart, and at the other of Ryman. White or black monochromes can be seen as a strategic moment of a constellation of practices of that period which push limit-cases to extremes. Such monochromes are the degree zero, hovering ambivalently on the aesthetic and institutional borders of the artworld, threatening to disappear into its very walls, and in so doing to make critically visible those walls. Constraints of space prevent us following this piece into the early seventies and the role of black and white in the work of this period. It must suffice here to say that *Camera* is a piece which most explicitly, and without the complex allegorical structures of, say, *Black Light*, illustrates the role of light as bright veil and dark shadow in photography; of exposure which reveals and concealing exposure.

CHIAROSCURO AND CHIASMUS

Exposure which reveals and concealing exposure is of course an example, if somewhat inelegantly forced, of the type of parallel syntactic inversion called 'chiasmus'. An equally apt, though rather less strained example, which is to be found in the Collins Dictionary, which John Hilliard owns, is "He stepped in, out stepped she". Both examples can be read as formulaic reductions of the operations of the photographs we have examined. Though the configurations and dynamics of whiteness and blackness, light and dark, has proved to offer a productive way in to these works, there is of course no single conclusion to be drawn, no summing up of what may have already come too close to a summing, to a kind of algebraic accounting. By way of conclusion, then, and to leave the last word, or last look, to the work itself, I have reproduced here two pieces which powerfully condense the themes and operations which we have been discussing, *Chiasmus* (1992) and *Exit* (1993) [refer to colour plates 9 and 10]. Both are visions of inverse reflection and reflections on the dynamics of vision, and both employ white and black light, costume, and props to effect chiaroscuro and chiasmus.

NOTES

1 *Philo*, (*On the Special Laws* 4.192), trans. F.H. Colson and G.H. Whitaker, Leob Classical Library, Heinemann, London, 1929-62.

2 Johan Wolfgang Von Goethe, *Theory of Colours*, trans. C. L. Eastlake, MIT Press, Cambridge, Mass.. 1970, pg. 7.

3 Issac Newton, *Opticks or a Treatise of the Reflections, Refractions, Inflections and Colours of Light* (1733), Dover, Mineola, 1952; See also, Rupert Hall, London, *All Was Light: an introduction to Newton's Opticks*, Clarendon Press, 1993.

4 Ludwig Wittgenstein, *Remarks on Colour*, ed. G.E.M. Anscombe, trans. Linda L. McAlister and Margaete Schattle, Blackwell, Oxford, 1978.

5. Richard Dyer, *White*, Routledge, London and New York, 1997, pp. 130-131.

6 Timothy Beardsworth, *A Sense of Presence: the phenomenology of certain kinds of visionary and ecstatic experience, based on a thousand first-hand accounts*, OUP, Oxford and New York, 1977.

7 *The Near-Death-Experience*, eds. Bailey and Yates, Routledge, London and New York, 1996.

8 *The Ray of Microcosm* (1845), trans, A. Savic-Rebac, *Harvard Slavic Studies 3*, 1957.

9 P. Rorem, *Pseudo-Dionysius: A Commentary on the Texts and An Introduction to their Influence*, OUP, Oxford and New York, 1993.

10 *The skull's Darkroom: The Camera Obscura and Subjectivity*, in 'Philosophy of Technology', Norman Kulwer Publishing, 1989.

11 Ibid.

12 Focus Works 1975/76, John Hilliard, Badischer Kunstvrein E.V. 1977, p. 9.

13 Arbeiten/Works 1990-96, John Hilliard, p. 16.

14 *Colour categories in thought and language*, ed. C.L. Hardin and Luisa Maffi, Cambridge University Press, Cambridge, 1997, p. 4.

15 Ibid., p. 5.

16 Jacques Lacan,*The Four Fundamental Concepts of Psycho-Analysis*, Norton, New York, 1981, p. 109.

17 Ibid., p. 109.

18 Andrew J. Webber,*The Doppelganger: Double Visions in German Literature*, OUP, Oxford and New York, 1996, p. 9.

19 Christian Metz, *Psychoanalysis and Cinema: the imaginary signifier*, Macmillian, London, 1982.

20 Jorge Luis Borges, *The Book of Sand*,

Penguin, London, 1979.

21 Ibid.

22 Otto Rank, *The Double: a psychoana-lytical study,* trans. Harry Tucker, Jr, Karnac, London, 1989.

23 Italo Zannier, "Fotografia: ossia credere nella verita: dal ritratto fisiogoico al ritratto fotometrico", in *Eidos.* 1991, no.9, p.59-68, on the shroud as an ideal for photographic portraiture, on the shroud as proto-photography see, the journal *History of Photography* (reference lost).

24 Jacques Derrida, "From Restricted to General Economy, A Hegelianism without Reserve" in, *Writing and Difference,* trans. Alan Bass, Routledge, London and New York, 1978.

25 *Vanitas, John Hilliard,* Wuttembergishe Kunstverein Stuttgart, 1990.

26 As of yet I have been unable to bring to light the reference for the article in which I originally found this argued, here, however, is another which may go some way towards supporting this argument: "Le Suaire de Turin aux prises avec l'histoire" in *Revue d'histoirede L'Eglise de France",* 1990, v.76, no.

196.

27 John Hilliard in *Arbeiten/works* 1990-96.

28 Ibid., p. 119.

29 Leon Battista Alberti, *On Painting,* Penguin, London, 1991.

30 Ibid., p. 130-131.

31 Michael Newman in ICA Catalogue, *John Hilliard,* 1984.

32 Herman Melville, *Moby-Dick,* www.americanliterature.com/MD/MD42.

33 John Hilliard in, *New Works 1981-1983.*

34 *The Impossible Document: photography and conceptual art in Britain 1966 – 197* ed. John Roberts, *Cameraworks, 1997,* p. 39.

IMAGE CREDITS

All images are reprinted from *John Hilliard, Vanitas,* Wurttembergischer Kunstverein, Stuttgart, 1990. Except *Chiasmus,* 1993 and *Exit,* 1994, from *John Hilliard, Works 1990-96,* Kunshalle Krems, Bozen, 1997. Used by permission of John Hilliard.

Lacan's *operational montage* from Jacques Lacan, *The Four Fundamental Concepts of Psycho-Analysis,* Norton Press, New York, 1981.

Literature
is like
phosphorous:
it shines
at its
maximum
brilliance at
the moment
when it
attempts to
die.

— Roland Barthes

[The phrases
 gallant gentleman
and the noblest
gentleman I know]
were to be applied
to Captain Oates
and his
companions.
Gentlemen in fact
not only knew how
gentleman should
behave, but how to
describe that
behaviour. The
event, inspiring
enough in itself,
was improved in
the telling.

— Mark Girouard

Where should one begin to look in interrogating the prestige of whiteness
in cinema? One could start with the white robes of the supremacist Klan
in *The Birth of a Nation* (Griffith, 1915), or the back lighting that creates a
halo of white light around Lillian Gish's hair in the same film. Whiteness
is a visual rhetoric of transcendental purity and bliss that even a
contemporary 'black filmmaker' like Steve McQueen resorts to in his short
film *Bear* (1993). Then there is Peter O'Toole's messianic white garb in
Lawrence of Arabia (Lean, 1961): an eroticized Christ leading the bickering
tribes to their Promised Land. Alternatively, there is the all-white cell of
Hannibal Lector in *Manhunter* (Michael Mann, 1986): clinical and
otherworldly, with undertones of institutional surveillance and the

inmate's *Übermensch*-like intellect. The wide-angle, deep-focus mise-en-scène of that film accentuates the monolithic and totalitarian aspects of white-cube International Style architecture to unsettling effect. Or, the opening and closing credits of Wong Kar-Wai's ironic and self-reflexive *Chungking Express* (1994), which are inversions of the orthodoxy of white letters on black screen. The black typography is scattered, Mallarmé-like, across the whiteness of the screen: the black-on-white of cinema's supposed opposite, writing.

White is the colour of both the empty screen and the blank page. In his book *Black Riders: The Visible Language of Modernism*, McGann argued that the actual technical process of printing black letters on white pages played an integral part in the development of Modernist language. The printed page becomes a work of art in the age of mechanical production; the architectonic of the text is poster art. Mallarmé, whose poems flaunt the silent whiteness of its pages, exemplifies this. As a direct reversal, the famous idiot savant speech spoken, by Lucky in *Waiting for Godot,* appears in print as an unpunctuated, unbroken mass of black letters devouring the white page: stream-of-consciousness as an unconsumable and unstoppable block of raw thought. To put it simplistically, writing can be seen as the tension and contention between black and white on the page.

The process and true nature of writing has been intensely debated and is beyond the scope of this paper. This is, however, a case study of writing as represented on the cinema screen, and the resulting implications for whiteness. The work focused on is *Scott of the Antarctic* (Charles Frend, 1948), and this film, I would like to propose, is at its heart about the power of language and writing: the compulsion to inscribe, to chart and to name; of drawing black trails upon white surfaces.

Structurally, *Scott of the Antarctic* is neatly divided into two halves: the first act details Scott's preparations for his second Antarctic expedition, the second act is the actual journey to the South Pole and back. Discounting the prologue, the first act has seventeen scenes. Significantly, all but one of them begin or conclude with a close-up of text, signs, printed message, the image of someone writing – one could say the film is *punctuated* by them. (A full run down of these images is listed in the appendix.) The whiteness of the film is not just that of the Antarctic, it is the whiteness of letters, journals, drawings, photographs and billboards. Granted, written text is an efficient way of relaying documentary information to the audience, and a few of the aforementioned images did exactly that, but a more conventional and seamless method is through expository dialogues. ("There you are, sir. The Great Ice Barrier. Four hundred miles long and a hundred foot high.") The film's fixation with written texts cannot be coincidental. After all, what finally survives from Scott's homeward march from the Pole is the journal that tells the tale of "hardihood, endurance, and courage [...] which would have stirred the hearts of every Englishman." The journal has become the totem of Scott's questionable heroism: the physical struggle has been condensed and represented by written language, which in turn becomes the vehicle of Scott's reputation and immortality. Conversely, if the text was lost in the snow, one could say Scott's efforts would have been totally in vain. In the last scene of the film, the journal is shown in a reverential close-up, its plain black cover resembling that of the Bible. As the men stand around the excavated camp and listen to the journal being read out in respectful silence, their heads bowed, the scene resembles a funeral or a mass: fittingly, for posthumous texts are the most revered.

Barthes' comparison of literature with burning phosphorous is an apt image of the historical pattern that hasthe strongest expression of a doctrine occuring at the end of its era. Scott's journey can be seen as poised at the moment when Romanticism begins to shift into Naturalism. What initially drives Scott's men forward is the abstract notion of the 'South Pole', a non-place gaining its meaning from Romantic language. The hermetic, quasi-masochistic behaviour of Scott and his crew are informed by the Romantic pursuit of the sublime: they read Tennyson and Coleridge on their journey, which double as scripts for their conduct. They are not "out for a bit of white ribbon" (as Scott says to Bowers in the film), but the "fame of virtue immortal" (Humphrey Gilbert). However, once Scott's party is beaten by Admundsen and the passion is gone, they remove the tinted lenses of Romanticism and see the prize for what it is: a barren wasteland. ("There is that curious damp feeling in the air that chills one to the bone. God, this is an awful place.") The return trip degenerates into the base reality of grime, frostbite and running sores.

'Taff' Evans, the strongman of the crew, dies of an untreated infection of his finger. Fearful of jeopardizing his chance of being selected on the final team to reach the Pole, he hastily covers the cut on his finger with a dirty glove to avoid Scott's inspection. This turns out to be his Achilles' heel. When Wilson subsequently cuts open the glove, we see the swollen hand in close-up. What is striking here is that death from infection and subsequent physical decline is a staple motif of the Naturalist fictions of Lawrence and Joyce, where squalid biology disrupts the veneer of chivalrous, gentlemanly respectability. Starting out with a Romantic script, Scott and his companions end up as characters in a Naturalist drama of deprivation and survival. These details are routinely overlooked in readings of the published journal by Scott's contemporaries: in perishing, Scott and his men fulfill the Romantic archetype, thus once more returning to the abstract, linguistic ideal.

The film's opening credits, shown after a prologue, are, interestingly enough, white letters on a blue screen: the blue of a presumably cloudless Antarctic sky, upon which bold, heroic white Roman letters (as employed by the white race?) are imprinted. There is then a shot of the ocean, panning up to a pair of buoys, which are themselves a kind of man-made mark on nature. Next comes the film's first image of writing. We see the black cover of a logbook, the white nametag bearing the inscription CAPT. R.F. SCOTT. On the top of the logbook lies another journal, open. A voiceover spoken by Scott (John Mills) himself has been heard from the beginning of the scene, it now begins to echo the handwritten text. The effect is half oration, half confession. This convention of voiceover accompanying journal entries will continue throughout the film, with one notable and effective exception. It is when Oates is seriously ill, and in a close-up we see Scott silently writes the words "Poor Soldier is at the end of his tether." The absence of voiceover paradoxically intensifies the confessional nature of the sentence, as if the fact is too demoralising to be spoken in public, and the writing is meant for our eyes only. It's a potent device for audience involvement in a film where conclusion is all but foretold.

We learn from the initiating voiceover/journal entry that Scott is returning from his first Antarctic expedition, but has only "touched the fringe of things". The layout of the last sentence on the page is as follows:

> I leave behind
> a whole Continent, – vast,
> Mysterious, Inhospitable and
> still to all intents and purposes
> unknown. —————-.

The long dash seems to symbolise the gap of knowledge and the vastness of the Antarctic that Scott craves: a distant horizon that holds promise. Scott's hand then enters the frame and empathetically adds a full stop – not the one at the end of the sentence, but the one immediately after the word 'unknown'. It is a strange and telling detail that visualises, by means of linguistic code, the foreclosure of Scott's first expedition: he was stopped short before accomplishing his march to the South Pole.

The film then slowly dissolves from the close-up of the journal to a grand view of the Antarctic, the whiteness of the page bleeding into the whiteness of the snowscape. For a moment, the two images are superimposed. It is as if the text is written directly onto the snow, or as if the black rocky structures that protrude from the blanket whiteness are a form of hieroglyphics too. With the benefit of hindsight, this stands out as the key image of the film. It stands for the desire to inscribe meaning onto the blank screen of whiteness, the passion of men who literally want to 'make their mark' upon the Antarctic, to impose the human will upon a timeless, uncharted, virginally white landscape. ("The fascination of making the first footmarks", as Scott said to his wife.) The footprints, flags, depots and huts are all trails of meaning imprinted on the whiteness, a sign system of human ambition, habit and travel. As the expeditionary ship cracks the Antarctic sea ice, lines of inky black are drawn over the flat white surfaces.

During the prologue the camera's point of view moves increasingly inland. It starts with a view of the Great Ice Barrier as seen from a ship: What is beyond it? What treasures lurk behind those dazzlingly white cliffs? With the camera/ship gently rocking, and a high-pitched, eerie female chorus on the soundtrack, the moment resembles a warped lullaby, a siren song that lures the seamen to their doom. The pristine beauty of white continent promises a white death. As the camera moves increasingly into the heart of the Antarctic, the white images are more picturesque and attractive, and hence more treacherous.

If the 'writing on Antarctica' shot is the key image of the film, then the dialogue between Scott and his wife at the end of the second scene is the film's key exchange. The scene begins with a close shot of a pensive Scott, accompanied by sentimental, melancholy string music. It is as if his passion with the Antarctic is a romance left unconsummated. Sure enough, Lady Scott adopts the curious language of a wife tolerating her husband's lingering affair with an old flame: "You knew the Antarctica before you knew me. I always knew you would go back, and I'm not the least jealous." Invigorated, Scott strides to his desk and composes his petition:

SCOTT   Now, what should it be... "I appeal with confidence" or "I confidently appeal"...

LADY SCOTT   "It is with confidence that we appeal."

A scene which appears to be a demonstration of matrimonial solidarity becomes in actuality a testimony to the power of writing and discourse. It makes plain that the characters are living in a society extremely conscious of the nuances of language, a world where seemly discourse supposedly boosts success, and phrasing is everything.

As befits a film preoccupied with language and writing, the first image of the film proper is a close-up of the word ADMIRALTY, as printed on a white bureaucratic form. The form itself is carried on a black lacquered tray, which is delivered into the office with a formally white-sleeved, black-jacketed hand. A disappointed Scott then walks out of the office and down the dirty, greyish corridors of power: the navy has lost its pristine white purity of purpose in failing to support Scott's second expedition.

As the film progresses, its preoccupation with the proper names of things becomes evident. When Wilson first appears, he is making a drawing of Natterer's Bat, a colourful designation that his wife comments on ("Lovely name.") and fondly repeats to herself in private ("Natterer's Bat, Natterer's Bat..."). The dogs and horses employed in the expedition are all given geographical (Hampstead) or anthropomorphic names ("...Wilson with Noddy, Oates with Christopher, and myself with Sibberts."), which makes their eventual execution all the more difficult. Moreover, whether as a nod to historical accuracy or a kind of original product placement, the brand names of Scott's equipment are repeatedly shown in close-ups. The speed dial on the expeditionary ship *Terra Nova* (a significant name in itself) is by W. BARTON & SONS ENGINEERS. EDINBURGH , and the automated piano in the Antarctic hut is courtesy of JOHN BROADWOOD & SONS. LONDON. Boxes of PETER DAWSON LTD. wines and OXO are displayed prominently in the expedition office.

Another moment of interest occurs when the expeditionary ship arrives at the Antarctic shore, and we see Scott writing the words CAPE EVANS (after 'Teddy' Evans, Scott's lieutenant in the expedition) on a previously unmarked area of the map. This is deemed a moment of urgency and import by the film. The image is accompanied by staccato strings and pounding, dramatic horns, and the completed inscription is held for a beat for us to contemplate. This naming of topological features is doubtlessly part of the attraction the expedition held for Scott. To be the first to reach an uncharted land is to be given the opportunity and power to name it, and in naming one assumes mastery over the subject. The act of naming not only promises individual fame, but is a symbolic triumph of colonialism.

In the final scenes, when Scott and his men are trapped in the snowstorm, it has become too difficult for them to write: fatigue and frostbitten fingers make the act laborious and painful. When it is physically impossible for them to write anymore, it's time to die. Scott's last words are, "It seems a pity, but I do not think I can write more. These rough notes, and our dead bodies, must tell the tale. For God's sake, look after our people." To give up writing is to surrender oneself to the existential, nullifying blank whiteness of the page, and by extension, that of the Antarctic. The epilogue of the film, describing the eventual recovery of Scott's remains by the search party, plays like a silent film; there are no more spoken words, and meaning is transmitted through body language and music. The very last shot of the film is a close-up of the engraved inscription TO STRIVE TO SEEK TO FIND AND NOT TO YIELD, then pans out to reveal the entire cross-shaped wooden headstone against the blue-white Antarctic sky.

––––––––

> It is not possible to sit back and 'watch' the story unfold, for one unconsciously finds one self taking part in their great risk, sharing their ordeal and privation, their triumph and bitter disappointments.

Thus goes the contemporary review of *Scott of the Antarctic* in *Monthly Film Bulletin*, January 1949. While the above statement is true, I would like to add an amendment. The suspension of disbelief – that is, the uncritical immersion in the text – is disrupted, particularly in the second half of the film, as a direct result of the predominate whiteness of the subject. The Antarctic is perceived as an infinite stretch of whiteness, while paradoxically boxed in by the boundaries of the frame and the darkness of the cinema. The viewer is thus acutely aware that he or she is watching a flat, white rectangular screen; the reflected light of which illuminates the auditorium. The dimmed auditorium conceals the viewer, retains privacy and encourages the dream-like experience of film; with the white light shining, one can see the expressions and reactions of fellow viewers, and vice versa. It is not so much a violation of the fourth wall as an indication of the actual materiality of film, and a reminder of the physical conditions of film viewing.

Whiteness in *Scott of the Antarctic*, together with its emphasis on written texts, is, whether conscious on the part of the filmmakers or not, a sign of the self-awareness of the film surface. The whiteness of the Antarctic snow, like the white robe of T. E. Lawrence, the white interiors in *Manhunter* or the white credits in *Chungking Express*, is a sure sign of a self-reflexive aesthetic drive. In the case of *Scott* this takes the form of a dawning historical revisionism and conceptual play with writing, of the compulsion to inscribe meaning upon white surfaces – the black on white, precisely, of the sentence you have just finished reading.

APPENDIX

Scene breakdown of the first half of *Scott of the Antarctic*, and notable images of writing appeared:

Prologue – insert: Scott's journal being written.

Scott at Naval office – begins with ADMIRALTY printed on bureaucratic form.

Scott and Lady Scott – ends with Scott writing petition.

Wilson, Oriana and Scott – begins with Wilson drawing Natterer's Bat.

British Antarctic Expedition office – begins with door sign; insert: application letters; ends with Scott naming dog Hampstead.

Scott's fundraising lecture – begins with billboard.

Scott and Oates – ends with Oates handing a cheque to Scott.

Scott and Nansen – begins with NORWAY caption and flag.

British Antarctic Expedition office –

begins with name plate, ends with budget chart.

Boarding the *Terra Nova* – begins with cover of Almunson's telegram to Scott.

Cabin – begins with piles of correspondences being opened.

Antarctic shore – ends with Scott writing CAPE EVANS on map.

Landing – begins with boxes printed BASE SHORE PARTY; insert: blueprint of hut.

Antarctica – begins with crew member writing geographical notes.

Scott's lecture to crew – insert: diagram of journey.

Polar Night – begins with crew writing microscopic findings.

Christmas party – begins with crossed-out calendar page.

Return of the Sun – ends with Ponting filming.

EPIGRAPHS

Roland Barthes, *Writing Degree Zero*, tr.
Annette Lavers and Colin Smith, Cape,
London, 1984.

Mark Girourd, *The Return to Camelot:
Chivalry and the English Gentleman,* Yale
University Press, New Haven and
London, 1981.

SEEING WHITENESS IN COLOUR
A CONSIDERATION OF SIGHTINGS: NEW PHOTOGRAPHIC ART

CHARLES RICE

Does an exhibition of colour photography have anything to contribute to
a seminar devoted to the issue of whiteness? Should it have anything to
contribute? Such questions immediately imply what is thought to be the
form of photography's automatic relevance, or correct relation, to the
cultural problematic of whiteness – the black and white photograph. It is
as if photography, thought about in its black and white manifestations,

would fit the language of cultural discussion implied by whiteness. This automatic, or correct relation, of the two perhaps only describes, or replays, the dynamics of giving over the correct form or historical manifestation of a cultural practice to a discussion about whiteness, rather than speculating as to the why of that giving over, the why of that automatic and unthought relation.

This essay will proceed on the premise that whiteness and photography have, and have had, automatic and unthought associations and implications in respect of each other, but instead of assuming or reactivating these associations, it will use the currency of the colour photography exhibition *Sightings: New Photographic Art*[1] to investigate the symbolic and historical undercurrents that lead to them.

The exhibition is deliberately chosen because it shows the wrong type of photographs for a discussion of whiteness, and is chosen in order to ask these questions: why is it wrong, and in what ways might it be right? What does the exhibition's cultural currency (the fact that it is on *now*) have to say about the significance *now* of a cultural problematic, whiteness, that may be seen initially to only have a particular, and in this sense automatic, way of relating to cultural events and practices?

This essay is an exercise to test in what ways the discourse of whiteness, itself formed from all types of symbolic and historical associations to cultural objects and practices, is capable of producing an account of this specific cultural event. Raymond Queneau's *Exercises in Style*[2] are taken as a model or analogy for this exercise. Queneau employs 99 different styles of language to describe the same short incident in 99 different ways. In a sense the incident is arbitrary, and the use of styles sets up a kind of structural rigour in language, but what results is a conjunction of language and incident that is more than the combination of arbitrariness and abstract rigour. These variations are in fact relations of synergy, combining the particular style of language employed and the incident as it inflects that style.

It may be possible to hypothesise whiteness as a style or, more usefully, a type or specific discourse in language, and to see how, what results from the description of a cultural event, becomes an exercise in language. But this analogy with Queneau also implies that there are other types of language that are able to relate the event of *Sightings*, and these would be the types of language used by curators, critics and other visitors. As with Queneau, these other exercises that might involve *Sightings* sit alongside this one.

Thus the exhibition is not *about* whiteness. The question is, rather, how can whiteness, as a particular use of language, describe it? The effectiveness of Queneau's method, which I hope to echo here, is that each exercise investigates simultaneously the significance of the type of language deployed and the richness of the event described. This exercise will begin with an evaluation of key images in *Sightings* as they are presented spatially and in sequence. These key images will structure a reading of certain key texts in photographic history in order to again approach the exhibition as a current comment on the outcome of this exercise.

THE SEQUENCE OF SIGHTINGS: INITIAL KEY IMAGES

The first image meets the eye when the viewer is effectively outside of the space of the gallery. Florence Paradeis' significantly titled *Blank* [refer to colour plate 11] is visible from the foyer of the Institute of Contemporary Arts. Its presence is first experienced before and outside of the exhibition proper. It shows a woman reaching under a white-sheeted bed. The white sheet forms a flat plane which occupies two thirds of the image from left to right. A sliver of a grey wall in the background defines the top of the bed, and the womans right arm is visible under the bed, running along the light grey floor beneath the sheet's hem. The woman's head is pressed against the side of the bed, her left hand gripping the leg of the bed through the sheet, the tension of her grip causing folds to radiate across the surface of the sheet from its lower right corner towards the top left of the image. The woman wears a black jumper, the sleeves of which are pushed up to her elbows, revealing her arms. Only her head, shoulders and arms are visible in the image. She has black hair. Her gaze is directed away from the force of her reaching, out of the image to the right hand side, and effectively out into the gallery. The momentum of one's trajectory entering the gallery takes one past this image and past her gaze to a series of images on the adjacent gallery wall.

Three images by Rineke Dijkstra are lined up on this white wall. The single figure in each photograph is framed against a white backdrop. Each photograph bears the title *Buzz (Club) Liverpool, England*, and three separate dates in March 1995. The figures in each photograph are girls dressed as for such a club. The middle photograph, *March 3*, pictures the girl approximately life size, centred and front on, cut off at knee level by the edge of the image [refer to colour plate 12]. She is wearing a dark green, navy and black tartan slip dress, the hemline reaching to lower thigh. The line of the tartan is diagonal. Her dark eyes stare directly at the camera, head slightly lowered and tilted to her left. Her bare shoulders and arms are only slightly darker in hue than the white backdrop. Her face is darker, being in a slight amount of shadow due to the angle of her head, as are the insides of her arms hanging straight down beside her dress. The visible part of her bare legs are darker still and show a fine web of blue veins. The hue of her legs is balanced by the dark straw-blond of her hair which reveals dark brown roots at the slightly off-centre parting. Her hair is pulled back, but two strands of wisps hang down over her face at either side of the front of the parting. These strands end below her chin at the whitest point of the upper part of her chest. She is holding a packet of cigarettes in her right hand, the middle finger of which has a ring. The cigarette packet, which is white on the outside edge with darker stripes closer to the palm of her hand, is balanced compositionally by a partly obscured white plastic hair clip that is visible at the top of her head on the left side of her parting.

Both these photographs described display an absence of strong colour, yet they are still colour photographs. In Paradeis' *Blank*, the colours are of ordinary furnishings, clothes and finishes – colours of choice. In Dijkstra's *March 3*, the colour makes evident that the cigarettes are a particular brand, the dress is a particular tartan, the hair colour is a particular chemical mix, all things chosen by the girl. The blue veins on her legs show she is cold.

The convention of *March 3* might be that of a studio portrait, but the intention of the girl's presence before the camera is ambivalent. She is not being photographed for herself, but neither does she, or the subjects of the other two of Dijkstra's photographs, appear shy. She knows why she is at the Buzz club (and she is dressed for it), but perhaps not why she is being photographed. In an essay accompanying the exhibition catalogue, Simon Morrissey notes that these girls in the *Buzz* series possess an autonomy equal to those that regard them.[3] This autonomy is in part granted by the heterogeneous nature of the images brought together in the exhibition. No particular style or school is represented in the collection of images; the very possibility of schools seems implausible for Morrissey given the equal validity of the images on display. This equal validity is then only constituted in formal terms. All that is able to be definitely accounted for are the formal qualities of each image.

Morrissey observes that this autonomy and formality is, however, situated within the everyday of experience, the sort of experience that involves dressing up and going to a nightclub, or reaching under a bed for something dropped or lost. This conjunction of formal autonomy and the everyday sets up a particular ambivalence both within the images themselves and the viewers relation to them as a collection. If the autonomy of the images implies the lack of an ability to fix a totalisable meaning for each image and the collection as a whole, how is one to account for this, given the very vividness of the reproduction techniques and the very recognisability of the content? If all one is able to give definitively is a formal description of the photographic surface, what is to be made of the familiarity of the detail that is photographed? What value do we give to the cigarettes, the hair clip, the blue veins of the girl in *March 3*, other than as part of the tonal composition to which they contribute?

The poles of this ambivalence fall either side of a distinction that can be made between the attributes of the photographed subject as against the attributes of the photographic surface. The hinge between the two is the question of colour, and whether we read it as belonging to the image surface or to the subject photographed. It should be quite easy to say, in looking at the *Sightings* exhibition, that the colours belonging to each are the same, or at least bear an indexical relation to one another, such is the quality of the reproduction of all the images. This is what one is led to believe in apprehending the initial key images described. But from photography's invention, the print, initially only black and white, was not thought about in relation to its colour fidelity or even its sharpness of detail in rendering its subject. Rather it came as a kind of proof of the objectivity and automatic nature of the picture taking process itself. The print's colour, or lack of it, belonged only to the print. What *Blank* and the *Buzz* series model so eloquently is the hint of this surface notion of black and white as incongruous behind the incredible colour fidelity of colour photographic techniques, such that the choice to photograph these subjects in colour must take on a particular significance. This choice could be described as a black and white effect in colour. In *Blank*, the only hues are black, white and grey, and the symbolic whiteness of the womans skin, modeled in the golden wood of the visible part of the beds leg. In *March 3*, the darkness of the tartan of the dress stands in for black, shown against a white ground, and the white skin and blonde hair in effect produce the gradation in tone (rather than a variation in colour) between white and black. This black and white effect calls directly to mind the history of black and white photography. But at the same time, the technical fact of the photograph's colour casts this calling to mind in a particular light, so to speak. What is at stake in these initial key photographs is the way they make evident, on the same photographic plane, the history of the conception of photography's technology and current techniques in photography, the rhetoric of black and white photography on the surface of the print, but on the same plane as the technique of colour photography that displays colour as the everyday choice and way of seeing of the subject.

BLACK AND WHITE IN PHOTOGRAPHIC HISTORY

In photography before the perfection of colour image fixing, there is a clear distinction between the colour attributes of the subject photographed and those of the photographic image simply because there was no relation between the two. The photographic image possessed no colour attributes, or if it did, they did not come about through an automatic process at the time of the exposure, and were in a sense the print's own colour. What came to be called black and white photography, which as a symbolic description encompasses also sepia and other monochrome tints, in fact describes the lack of variant colour on the image surface that would relate directly to the subject photographed. In the history of what is called black and white photography, black and whiteness becomes linked to technical rather than aesthetic considerations, to achromatic rather than chromatic values.

André Bazin is significant in this context as he precisely draws a distinction between technical and aesthetic aspects in photography that hinge on the question of resemblance between image and subject photographed, most significantly the human subject. He says that the impetus for preserving a bodily appearance, firstly by embalming the body itself (as in Egyptian mummification) and then its image through what would later become thought of as the function of art, fulfills the psychological need to overcome death.[4]

In considering painting, Bazin contends that this psychological aspect of art became more evident than its symbolic, or what he terms its aesthetic function, with a technical invention, which Bazin describes as the first scientific and already, in a sense, mechanical system of reproduction, namely perspective: the camera obscura of Da Vinci foreshadowed the camera of Niépce.[5] Bazin continues:

> henceforth painting was torn between two ambitions: one, primarily aesthetic, namely the expression of spiritual reality wherein the symbol transcended its model; the other, purely psychological, namely the duplication of the world outside... Nevertheless, the fact remains that we are faced with two essentially different phenomena and these any objective critic must view separately if he is to understand the evolution of the pictorial.[6]

The illusion of likeness given in painting was reckoned sufficient unto art. Photography and cinema, on the other hand, are discoveries that satisfy, once and for all in its very essence, our obsession with realism.[7] In this way, photography frees the plastic arts from the burden of imitation and the production of likeness.

This argument is interesting, not for its inherent truth about realism, but for this as a conceptualisation of the photographic apparatus at a particular historical moment. Bazin found photography's technical genesis in the plastic arts, but at the point at which the apparatus of the camera becomes able to fix an image automatically, it becomes something different from what had come to be known as the plastic arts. It completes the psychological project of the plastic arts, a project at their very heart, and frees them to pursue what is termed the aesthetic project, always linked to the subjectivity of the artist, a subjectivity absent, so says Bazin, from the image making technique of the photographic camera. The aesthetic project is also a project of the relation between form and colour. The liberation of painting allowed by photography, enabling painting to recover its aesthetic autonomy, is a freedom to use colour in a non-imitative fashion.

Only when form ceases to have any imitative value can it be swallowed up in colour. So, when form, in the person of Cézanne, once more regains possession of the canvas, there is no longer any question of the illusions of the geometry of perspective.[8]

The key to the completion of the psychological project of the plastic arts for Bazin is not to be found in the result achieved, but in the way of achieving it.[9] Thus the satisfaction of the desire for realism stems not from a photograph looking any more real than a painting of the same object, rather it stems from the fact that the photograph is believed to be automatic. This has significant implications for the status of the photograph as an object, because it is at this historical period that realism in photography becomes associated with the objective technology of photography, its metonym being the lense which determines its objective character, which is literally, the character of the lense. The black and whiteness of the images themselves is a function of the technology, and not the primary object of belief in itself. Explaining the role of the image further, Bazin says that the photographic image is bound to its object, both sharing a common being, after the fashion of a fingerprint.[10] The black and whiteness of the photograph has, like the ink bearing a fingerprint, no significance in and of itself. It is, however, inseparably associated with the object whose image it bears, just as the ink bears the fact that it is a print of a finger that has touched it. Bazin says that it is this category of resemblance that determines, or rather is, the aesthetic of the photograph as distinct from the aesthetic of painting, which could loosely be termed artistic in its identification with beauty: the perfection of a reproduction is not to be identified with beauty. It constitutes rather the prime matter, so to speak, on which the artistic fact is recorded.[11]

The perfection of the photograph's representation is not artistic but factual, and its black and whiteness is the prime matter of this factuality. Black and whiteness is itself not representative of anything, except it is that which defines the figure in the black and white image. In doing such it is inseparable from the technology by which the resemblance is produced, and to which the discourse on realism refers. Black and whiteness is *given* the association with realism as the function of a technology conceptualised at a particular historical moment when black and white was the most advanced state of that technology.

For Walter Benjamin however, the human figure as a subject still confuses the relation of photography and painting. His discussion of the relation between painting and photography hinges on the genre of the portrait, and he sees the early discourse on photography's maintenance of artistic codes and genres as a historically regressive moment in the development of thought about both photography and art. Far from immediately freeing art from the burden of resemblance, photography, for the most part, perished into art by maintaining an obsession with the portrait: the renunciation of the human image is the most difficult of all things for photography.[12] It is, Benjamin contends, an anti-technological and literally conservative view of art that has made practitioners of photography repeat the forms and canons of established art practice. It is photography's capability for technical development beyond art in this sense that has been feared, but that is also photography's promise according to Benjamin. The technology of photography brings with it a change in apperception, a change in one's consciousness of perception. It is a different nature which speaks to the camera than speaks to the eye.[13] Benjamin called this different nature the means by which one learns of what he termed the "optical unconscious".[14] The photograph makes visible those things passed over, or not directly seen, in normal perception, those things in the world only known unconsciously: the posture of the body frozen in motion, or the enlargement of a plant's cell structure that take resemblance to a level beyond the moody landscape or the soulful portrait.[15] The equivalent of this effect is in the technology's ability to show people in front of the camera who were not being photographed for their own purposes. And suddenly the human face entered the image with a new, immeasurable significance. But it was no longer a portrait. What was it?[16]

It was not a way of seeing new things, but a new way of seeing. Thus Benjamin can be seen to extend Bazin's concept of the psychological desire for realism by putting it a different way. The technology of the photographic camera opens up to ordinary sight via the photographic print an unconscious relation to the real world, by modelling the action of what Benjamin thinks must be our unconscious perception of reality. Both accounts of the psychological basis and impact of photography's effects hinge on the camera as a technological apparatus. It is now possible to say, after Benjamin, that it is the photographic print that is literally the proof of the technology, and the possibilities for its reproduction that fundamentally recast our relation to art and our conception of its possible subjects and functions.[17] The impact on our psychology of the photographic print (and here Benjamin and Bazin include the moving image), moves out of the realm of the aesthetics of the artistic image and towards the social function of images.

> It is significant that the debate becomes stubborn chiefly where the aesthetics of *photography as art* are involved, while for example the much more certain social significance of *art as photography* is hardly accorded a glance. And the effect of photographic reproduction of works of art is of much greater importance for the function of art than the more or less artistic figuration of an event which falls prey to the camera.[18]

It is clear that the reproducibility of images, and hence the possibility of a social function for art, relies on their black and whiteness as once again a technical consideration.

The arguments of Bazin and Benjamin implicate the black and whiteness of the image, though in an almost unspoken fashion. For Bazin the image is not so much the object's likeness as the proof of its being, its reality.

The photographic image is the object itself, the object freed from the conditions of time and space that govern it. No matter how fuzzy, distorted, or discoloured, no matter how lacking in documentary value the image may be, it shares, by virtue of the very process of its becoming, the being of the model of which it is a reproduction. It *is* the model.[19] For Benjamin, the reality of the model, which for the first time could be an unintended subject, the person in the street, is in its manipulability. In talking about the possibility for the photographic reproducibility of paintings, Benjamin says:

> One can no longer view them as the productions of individuals; they have become collective images, so powerful that the capacity to assimilate them is related to the condition of reducing them in size. In the final effect, the mechanical methods of reproduction are a technology of miniaturisation and help man to a degree of mastery over the works without which they no longer are useful.[20]

Bazin's metaphor of the photograph as fingerprint is an apt one in light of the degree of mastery that photographs supply for Benjamin.

Thus attributes of the image can be established which in turn establish the characteristics of photographic black and whiteness as a function of the technology of the camera. The black and whiteness of the image cannot be thought about in relation to the colour of the subject photographed but rather records the subject technically, as a fact. Black and whiteness is the proof of a lack of subjectivity in the image fixing process. It is the manifestation of a level of perception that is not that of our eyes which see in colour. It is a level of perception that makes the eye aware of what perception involves unconsciously. This unconscious is also the basis of a deeper level of belief, and the fact of black and whiteness is seen as the reality and the fulfillment of the desire for this. Black and whiteness is not part of an aesthetic of painting, its nearest artistic cousin, but it can give painting a reproducibility that changes this aesthetic function and turns it into a social function by reducing the images singularity and enabling its wide circulation. Black and whiteness can also free painting to deal with form in an entirely different manner, a manner, in the final instance, that hinges on the use of colour.

What must be grasped is the historical specificity of these arguments. It is only after Bazin and Benjamin that colour in photography has become an issue. They seem to take us up to a particular historical moment in the development of the technology of the camera, which does not technically go beyond black and white. But this historical specificity is not quite so sound in terms of the issue of colour in photography, especially in Bazins case, who published *The Ontology of the Photographic Image* in 1945, four years after the invention and use of Kodacolour negative film, and nine years after Benjamin wrote his *Short History of Photography*.

COLOUR IN PHOTOGRAPHIC HISTORY

Even before the technical reality of colour photography a discourse about colour and its relation to the photographic apparatus had in fact shadowed the development of the apparatus, but had lagged behind considerably in terms of the development of its technical applicability. Early in his photographic investigations, Niépce remarked: "I must succeed in fixing the colours", and in 1827 he and Daguerre discussed this, but it was discovered that monochrome daguerrotypes would provide more immediate possibilities. In 1850 American Levi Hill obtained coloured daguerrotypes from an accidental combination of chemicals that he was unable to rediscover.[21] Coloured images were projected by James Clerk Maxwell in London in 1861 in a process of additive colour mixing by the conjunction of three coloured slides taken of the same subject. John Joly produced what is said to be the first colour photographic image seen without the aid of an apparatus in Dublin in 1893. This was the beginning of the subtractive colour process that led to the Lumière brother's glass autochrome plates in 1903 and subsequently, through various manifestations, to the Kodachrome film of 1935 and the Kodacolour negative film of 1941.[22] But all the while the technical ascendancy of black and white prints became associated with a sought after abstract truth. Colour, like excessive detail, was felt to be a disadvantage in [photographic] art because it never failed to suggest the indiscriminate vulgarity of everyday life.[23] The emergence of colour in artistic and documentary photographic practice did occur with Eliot Porter and Ernst Haas in the late forties and fifties. Porter was interested in the colour qualities of natural scenes, and Haas used techniques such as double exposures and altered exposure times to produce particular colour effects.[24] Graham Clark comments that Porter and Haas effectively make the colour of the image surface the subject of their work, in this way intensifying the presence of the actual photographic subject.[25] They were followed by a series of new colour photographers in the seventies and eighties, notable among them being William Eggleston. In a catalogue for an exhibition of these new colour photographers, Sally Eauclaire, in a significant tack away from the concerns of Porter and Haas, traces the antecedents for the work not from what she calls these old colour photographers, but from the renewed interest in the late sixties for Eugène Atget and Walker Evans. Antecedents for the use of colour she traces to the influence of modern painting.[26] The new colour photographers assimilated the overall principles of modern painting from the Impressionists onward.[27] She, in opposition to Clark, contends that the conception of the photographic surface comes to be thought of separately from a desire to intensify the presence of the images antecedent. In a similar fashion, Eugenia Parry Janis, in writing on an exhibition of colour polaroids by photographic artists, states that colour's greatest moments occur in the arts of non-representation.[28] In her assessment of the work, Janis suggests that its significant aspect involves a process of assembling colours compositionally before taking a picture. It is in this fashion that she speaks of an evolving photographic colour consciousness that has emerged following a reluctance by photographic artists to use colour because of its dominance of photographic advertising.[29]

It is evident from the history of colour in photography that the relation of painting and photography once again becomes an issue even within the historical time and historically traced arguments of Benjamin and Bazin, and it rests on more than just the aesthetic freeing up of the former by the latter, or the reproducibility of the former by the latter.

Looking back at Bazin's tracing of the history of the photographic camera from the camera obscura, it is possible to see his argument being shadowed by a discourse on colour that is also tied to the apparatus of the camera obscura and the development of Renaissance painting, but that now only makes sense in terms of colour photography as the most advanced position of photographic technology. And in being such, it brings back arguments that Bazin and Benjamin excluded from their accounts of the psychology of the photograph on account of the fact that photography was, for them, then dominant and effective only as a black and white technology.

What is brought back most profoundly in the history of colour and photography is the relation of colour to the conception and applicability of the camera obscura in painting. In his treatise *On Painting*, and in relation to his arguments about the applicability of the camera obscura, Alberti speaks of four genera of colours that relate in turn to the four elements of nature. Red is the colour of fire, blue of the air, green of the water, and of the earth grey and ash. Therefore there are four genera of colours and these make their species according to the addition of dark or light, black or white.* Alberti links black and white with dark and light, the latter being the role shadow and light plays in changing the perceptual attributes of colour. Alberti is suggesting that the painter is able to mix an infinite array of colours on the palette for application to the canvas, mimicking the play of light and shadow in the real world. He suggests:

> White and black are not true colours but alterations of other colours. The
> painter will find nothing with which to represent the brightest lustre of
> light but white and in the same manner only black to indicate the
> shadows. I should like to add that one will never find black and white
> unless they are mixed with one of these four colours.[30]

Black and white are thus a function of light, the very proof of the black and white photographic image as being a fixing of form by an automatic writing with light, but a proof that is not available before the camera obscura can fix a print. The nature of the photographic image as being

black and white is here prefigured to the same extent as the technology of
the photographic camera is prefigured by the camera obscura. But
Albertis black and white are always coloured black and white, only seen in
relation to an effect on colour, either the brightest white of light bleaching
colour, or the deepest shadow dampening it. Black and white is there
unconsciously for Alberti, not visible in essence, but it is made visible to
normal perception in the black and white photographic print, at once
changing a consciousness of perception and as such fulfilling a desire for
realism.

SIGHTINGS AGAIN

This notion and effect of black and white is mixed into colour again, with
the advent of colour photography, but only after black and white has set a
way of thinking about photography and changed the nature of our
perception of the world through it. But there are two ways of thinking
about colour in relation to colour photography, overlaid and always
present with each other in the colour image. In the Albertian sense, colour
is the bearer of the black and whiteness that is the unconscious truth
made evident first in the black and white photograph. In the sense of the
use of colour in modern painting, colour came to be thought of as being
able to be free of figurative resemblance, and being a subject in its own
right, in the sense of Bazin's invocation of Cézanne and the discourse
surrounding photographic practice in the seventies and eighties. Coming
back to the concerns expressed initially in respect of Paradeis' *Blank* and
Dijkstra's *Buzz* series, it is possible to see an Albertian concept of colour
as the historical trajectory of the black and white effect of these colour
photographs, a trajectory passing through the history of photographic
technology. Black and white echoes historically beneath the colour, in
terms of a reading of the formal composition of the image, but as a
colour photographic image, what is this effect as more than a historical
relation? Although this historical relation sets up a frame wherein one may
feel surer in starting to understand these images in light of a greater

knowledge about a distinction between aesthetic and psychological ascriptions and determinants in terms of colour and black and white, the story within the exhibition is much more complex. What is the effect of this knowledge across other images in the exhibition? In what sense can Dijkstra's and Paradeis' images be construed, along with the historical significance which they reveal, as key images for understanding the *Sightings* exhibition as the current state of colour photographic art?

It is perhaps by a combination of factors, by the actual placement of the images that was emphasised earlier, and by thinking about how the historical association was unlocked in them. To reprise their earlier description, it was a question of colour seeming to belong to the surface and to the subject simultaneously that lead to their ambivalent, but compelling presence. The significance of these images black and whiteness emerged from considering black and whiteness as being only an attribute of the images surface, and not of the subject, but what was found in that historical relation had implications for thinking about the plastic attributes of colour as also having a surface effect, as well as a relation to the subject. Thus colour now straddles the ambivalence between image surface and the subjects depth.

Several images in the exhibition instil this ambivalence by answering to both aspects of colour, that is, colour in the Impressionist and Albertian sense. Miles Coolidge's two *Central Valley* photographs emphasise only breath. The flatness and featurelessness of the farming landscape is in effect analogised by the photographs 1:12.7 dimensions. This flatness is reinforced by the grain of the colour, nearing pointilism, and the suspicion that this way of applying colour to the figuration of the landscape could continue independently of the need to expose a photographic film to light. And in the upper gallery, in a sense at the end of the exhibitions trajectory, is Jorg Sasse's *5671*, an equally flat and grainy image of a large modern tenement building, seemingly adrift in a sandstorm that obscures the nature of the buildings connection with the ground. The closer one goes to this image, the flatter and more painterly

it becomes. But right next to Sasse's image are two *Untitled* images by
Hannah Starkey that show a depth of colour and light that are painterly in
their richness but also cinematic in their scale and dimensions.

The technical question of photography arises in an interesting way
when considering Coolidge and Sasse images. How were they made? Must
ones understanding of the technology of photography change in order to
accommodate their use of colour? This questions any certainty or solace
we might have read in regarding Starkeys images, since they are in this
same exhibition, too. They are part of the same technical medium. Black
and white emerges even here, in the most self-consciously colourful of
the images, as the certainty of what it has historically described about the
objective and automatic nature of photographic technology becomes
completely uncertain.

CONCLUSION

Thus the argument has returned to the initial question of ambivalence and
whether the sense of photography can be neatly divided between
questions of technology in respect of black and white images, and
aesthetics in respect of colour images. But here, ambivalence is not a sign
of interpretative weakness or curatorial caprice, but is historically
inscribed in the discourse on the technological and aesthetic development
of photography. This ambivalence arose from finding a whiteness in the
first key images, then naming that historically as black and whiteness, this
history then being allied with an understanding of the technical truth of
the apparatus. The particular time of the historical accounts given,
particularly Bazin's, then hinted at the exclusion of colour as a technical
development, and a whole history of colour and photography emerged
that refigured the conception of the technology along chromatic lines.
This aspect was underscored by several more key works in *Sightings* that
used colour to highlight questions of photographic technique.

In light of the trajectory of this argument, it is worth again
considering it as an exercise. Whiteness as a type of language emerged in

this argument as one initially of formal description. As such whiteness took on the significance of black and whiteness in relation to tonal values. This black and whiteness became a rhetoric in its being overlaid with colour as a black and white effect, which in turn was invoked as constituting the historical understanding of the technology of photography. At the emergence of the technical reality of colour photography, a critique of the surety of how photographic technology is understood arose, a surety with which whiteness, inflected as black and whiteness, was historically complicit.

But whiteness has not failed in giving an account of *Sightings*. It has not failed because it was worked through in relation to colour photography, rather than being simply and initially accepted or rejected by a category of automatic association. In a sense it showed the history of how such an automatic association can become entrenched, and how an association can be thought wrong. The only automatic limitation was imposed at the beginning, by treating whiteness as a type of language, a manner of speaking. This limitation might prove useful to thinking about its elusive character as a possible description of cultural practices. The reason for the limitation was because the discourse of whiteness can be thought of as always a test of language, an exercising of it, rather than being a whole language in itself. It thus only emerges in things, in its description of events, its breadth and applicability only able to be judged in relation to the conjunction, following Queneau, of incident and style, and again in relation to 98 other styles of description.

This manner of thinking about whiteness can also be figured in terms of its appearance in images. Three images by Elisa Sighicelli figure whiteness within the *Sightings* exhibition in a particular way. *Curtain, Las Vegas Curtain* and *Table* are partially backlit colour photographs. These images are not hung together, but are placed at particular positions throughout the exhibition, effectively punctuating one's experience of it. The light of the light boxes on which they are mounted shines through a window in each image, a curtained window in the first two images and an opaque window in the last, producing a luminous white surface. The whiteness of this surface is not the light itself, but the means by which it is diffused and forms on the image a luminous white. By analogy, a manner of speaking is the way language is diffused. A discourse on whiteness comes about by the particular way language is used and diffused. Thus even in this analogy between image and discourse, the event that is *Sightings* has an equal claim to the resulting story produced by its conjunction with a manner of speaking.

NOTES:

1 *Sightings: New Photographic Art*, 10 January - 15 March 1998, Institute of Contemporary Arts, London, curated by Tim Dawson.

2 Raymond Queneau, *Exercises in Style*, trans., Barbara Wright, Gaberbocchus Press, London, 1958.

3 Simon Morrissey, "The end is the beginning is the end" in *Sightings: New Photographic Art*, ICA, London, 1998, n.p.

4 André Bazin, "The Ontology of the Photographic Image" in *What is Cinema? Volume 1*, ed. and trans. Hugh Gray, University of California Press, Berkeley, 1967, p. 9.

5 Ibid. p. 11.

6 Ibid.

7 Ibid. p. 12.

8 Ibid. p. 16.

9 Ibid. p. 12.

10 Ibid. p. 15.

11 Ibid.

12 Walter Benjamin, "A Short History of Photography", trans. Phil Patton, in *Classic Essays on Photography*, ed. Alan Trachtenberg, Leetes Island Books, New Haven, Conn., 1980, p. 210.

13 Ibid. p. 202.

14 Rosalind Krauss understands the psychoanalytic implication of the term optical unconscious in a way that I think is different from what Benjamin has intended. She takes Benjamin to mean that photography is the unconscious for a personified notion of the visual field. My use of the term here takes Benjamin to mean that photography provides a visual way of understanding what is not perceivable or understood in terms of a person's conscious sight. It is therefore unconscious in a descriptive sense, but not without a resonance with some of the psychological arguments made by Bazin. See Rosalind Krauss, *The Optical Unconscious*, MIT Press, Cambridge, Mass. and London, 1993, p. 178-179.

15 Benjamin, "A Short History of Photography", p. 203.

16 Ibid. p. 210.

17 Benjamin's meditation on this aspect of photography is to be found in: "Walter Benjamin, The Work of Art in the Age of Mechanical Reproduction", in *Illuminations*, ed. Hannah Arendt, trans. Harry Zohn, Fontana, London, 1992, pp. 211-244.

18 Benjamin, "A Short History of Photography", p. 211.

19 Bazin, "The Ontology of the Photographic Image", p. 14.

20 Benjamin, "A Short History of Photography", p. 212.

21 Beaumont Newhall, *The History of Photography, From 1839 to the Present Day*, revised and enlarged ed., MoMA, New York, 1971, p. 191. The names and dates that follow are taken from ibid., pp. 191-194.

22 Newhall gives the date of Kodacolour negative film becoming available as 1941 (ibid., p. 193.), but this is contradicted in two other sources which both give the date as 1942. These sources are: Mike Weaver, ed., *The Art of Photography, 1839-1989*, Yale University Press, New Haven and London, 1989, p. 5; and Graham Clarke, *The Photograph*, Oxford University Press, Oxford and New York, 1997, p. 237.

23 Mike Weaver, "Prologue: The Picture as Photograph", in *The Art of Photography, 1839-1989*, ed. Mike Weaver, Yale University Press, New Haven and London, 1989, p. 10.

24 See Newhall, *The History of Photography*, p. 194.

25 Graham Clark, *The Photograph*, Oxford University Press, Oxford and New York, 1997, p. 179.

26 Sally Eauclaire, *New Color / New Work: Eighteen Photographic Essays*, Abbeville Press, New York, 1984, pp. 10-12.

27 Ibid. p. 10.

28 Eugenia Parry Janis, "A Still Life Instinct: The Colour Photographer as Epicurean", in *One of a Kind: Recent Polaroid Color Photography*, ed. Belinda Rathbone, David R. Goldine, Boston, 1979, p. 14.

29 Ibid. p. 12-13.

30 Leon Battista Alberti, *On Painting*, trans. John R. Spencer, revised ed., Yale University Press, New Haven and London, 1966, p. 50.

IMAGE CREDITS

Florence Paradeis, *Blank*, ICA Publishing, London, 1998. Reprinted by permission of Florence Paradeis.

Rineke Dijkstra, *Buzz (Club) Liverpool, England, March 3, 1995,* ICA Publishing, 1998. Reprinted by permission of Museum Boijmans Van Beuningen. Copyright Rineke Dijkstra.

BIOGRAPHIES

Ruth Adams was awarded a first class honours degree in Sociology and Visual Culture from Lancaster University. She currently is working at the Royal Society of Arts, and is researching her doctorate on the professionalisation of museum work in post-war London.

Kathy Battista received her B.A. in Art History and English Literature from Fordham University and M.A. in Art History from the Courtauld Institute of Art. She is Head of Interaction at Artangel and co-author of Recent Architecture in the Netherlands (1998) and Art New York (2000). She is currently researching feminist artists in seventies London.

Christopher Hight is an architect and designer, and is a recipient of a Fulbright Scholarship, the AIA School Medal and the Alpha Roe Chi Medal. He has practiced in the United States and as a member of the Renzo Piano Building Workshop. He teaches in the Graduate Design Research Laboratory at the Architectural Association, where he also earned a Masters degree with Distinction .

Lorens Holm is a practising architect and teaches theory at the Bartlett School of Architecture. Before coming to London, he was Assistant Professor of Architecture at Washington University in St. Louis. He is currently writing on problems of space, perception, and representation in architecture and psychoanalytic theory.

Travis Miles was educated in Twin Falls, Idaho and Swarthmore, Pennsylvania. His research interests include documentary, cinema maudit, animation and Jean-Pierre Leaud. In June of 2000, he was the co-organiser (with Michael Uwemedimo) of the international conference, Possessing Vision: The Cinema of Jean Rouch, at the Institute of Contemporary Arts.

Mark Morris trained at Ohio State University where he received the American Institute of Architects Medal for Excellence in the Study of Architecture. He has published articles in the U.S., U.K., Italy and Germany. Recently awarded a Royal Institute of British Architects grant, his doctoral research focuses on scale models.

Charles Rice teaches architecture at the University of New South Wales in Sydney, Australia, and has previously taught in General Studies at the Architectural Association. His research focuses on notions of the image in architectural discourse and practice.

David Tang received his B.A. in English and the History of Art from University College London. He has worked for the BBC World Service, Sight and Sound Magazine, and in 1997 won the Anne Frankel Award for Best Young Film Critic.

John Tercier is a specialist in emergency medicine. He is currently researching representations of science in popular culture.

Michael Uwemedimo holds a B.A. in Humanities from Birkbeck College and is a lecturer at that institution. His current work is on mimesis and intoxication. He is curating a festival of non-fiction film and a retrospective of the works of Godard at the NFT and Tate Modern.

Diana Yeh graduated from King s College London with a B.A. Honours in French before completing the London Consortium s M.Res. in Humanities and Cultural Studies. She currently works as a writer and editor.

COLOPHON

Designed by Christopher Hight
with Lorens Holm and Mark
Morris.

Set in distorted Helvetica and
Garamond.

Printed by Cambridge University
Press

A NOTE ON THE DESIGN

The design operates upon the
rules which have organised book
design in modernity. It does not
pretend to simply replace these
systems but to operate upon their
logic until the breaking point and
with as little 'design' as possible.
Rather than a minimalism of
purification this is achieved by
dirtying these structures by
intensifying and multiplying their
ordering. Similarly, following
Mallarmé, the white page is
considered not as the neutral nor
moreover, gridded, ground upon
which the figures of text and
image play, but as a supple,
directional field within which text
and image are embedded and
feedback.

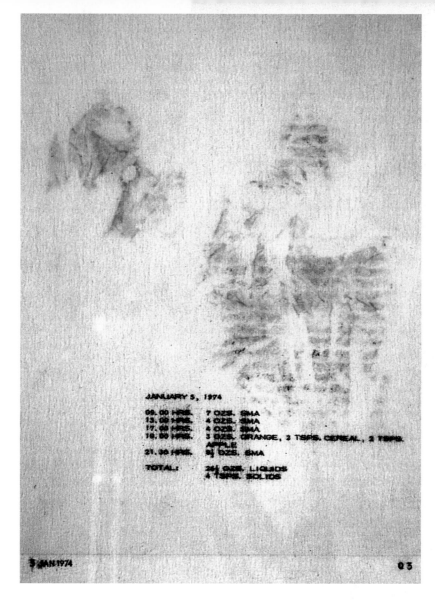

Colour Plate 1
Mary Kelly, *Post-Partum Document, Documentation 1,* 1973

C O L O U R   P L A T E S

Above:
Colour Plate 2
South Elevation of Tate Gallary with Shrapnel Damage

Right and overleaf:
Colour Plate 3, 4, 5
Shrapnel Damage

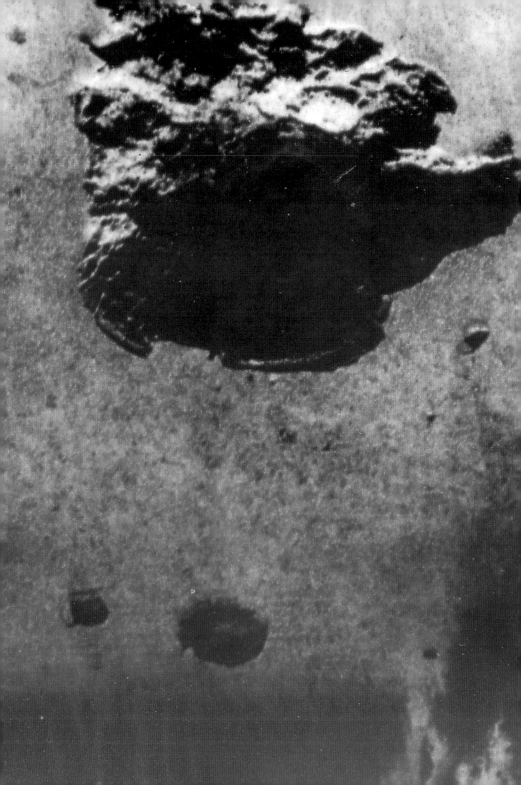

Colour Plate 6:
John Hilliard, *I see a black light*, 1987

Colour Plate 7:
John Hilliard, *Masquerade*, 1982

Colour Plate 8:
John Hilliard, *Facade*, 1982

Colour Plate 9:
John Hilliard, *Chiasmus*, 1992